STOP F*CKING TALKING AND START LISTENING:

MASTERING ACTIVE LISTENING TO BECOME A BETTER COLLEAGUE, FRIEND, AND PARTNER

JD VAUGHN

CONTENTS

Introduction   5

1. FOUNDATIONS OF ACTIVE LISTENING   7
   1.1 The Art of Empathy in Listening   7
   1.2 Building Emotional Intelligence for Better Listening   9
   1.3 Cultivating Self-Awareness Through Active Listening   10
   1.4 The Role of Mindfulness in Enhancing Listening   12
   1.5 Creating Trust with Every Conversation   14

2. OVERCOMING LISTENING BARRIERS   16
   2.1 Managing Emotional Reactions for Clearer
   Communication   18
   2.2 Focus and Presence: The Art of Staying Engaged   20
   2.3 Breaking Down Cultural Barriers in Listening   21
   2.4 Navigating Listening Blocks and Distractions   23

3. NONVERBAL COMMUNICATION MASTERY   25
   3.1 Facial Expressions: Reading Between the Lines   27
   3.2 Understanding Gestures Across Cultures   29
   3.3 Posture and Proximity: Unspoken Elements of
   Interaction   30
   3.4 Enhancing Digital Communication with Nonverbal
   Cues   32

4. PRACTICAL EXERCISES FOR LISTENING
   IMPROVEMENT   34
   4.1 Empathy-Building Activities for Personal Growth   36
   4.2 The Feedback Loop: Practicing Constructive
   Dialogue   38
   4.3 Listening Journals: Tracking Progress and Insights   39
   4.4 Interactive Scenarios: Applying Skills in Real Life   41

5. ADVANCED TECHNIQUES FOR DIALOGUE BALANCE   45
   5.1 Open-Ended Questions: Encouraging Deeper
   Dialogue   47
   5.2 Echoing and Paraphrasing: Techniques for
   Clarification   48
   5.3 Managing Dominance and Reticence in Group
   Settings   50
   5.4 The Art of Silence in Communication   52

6. DEVELOPING EMPATHY AND UNDERSTANDING 54
   6.1 Emotional Resonance: Connecting Beyond Words 56
   6.2 Building Rapport Through Reflective Listening 57
   6.3 Trust and Vulnerability in Conversations 59
   6.4 Navigating Difficult Emotions with Compassion 60

7. DIGITAL LISTENING AND VIRTUAL
   COMMUNICATION 63
   7.1 Text-Based Conversations: Reading Between the
   Lines 65
   7.2 Managing Multitasking in Digital Communication 66
   7.3 Creating Presence in Virtual Meetings 68
   7.4 Tools and Technologies for Enhanced Digital
   Listening 70

8. BUILDING CUSTOMIZED LISTENING PLANS 72
   8.1 Assessing Your Listening Habits and Challenges 72
   ■ Strengths (What's Working?) 74
   ■ Weaknesses (What's Challenging?) 74
   ■ Opportunities (How Can You Improve?) 75
   Threats (What Could Derail Your Progress?) 75
   8.2 Setting Realistic Goals for Listening Improvement 76
   8.3 Tailoring Techniques to Your Unique Needs 77
   8.4 Creating a Supportive Environment for Practice 79
   8.5 Monitoring Progress and Adjusting Plans 80

9. EXPERT INSIGHTS AND REAL-LIFE APPLICATIONS 83
   9.1 Real-Life Case Studies: Success Stories in Listening 85
   9.2 Overcoming Professional Listening Challenges 86
   9.3 Applying Active Listening in Conflict Resolution 88
   9.4 Insights from Therapeutic Listening Practices 89

10. LIFELONG LEARNING AND REFLECTIVE PRACTICE 92
   10.1 Reflective Practice: Learning from Every Interaction 94
   10.2 The Future of Listening: Adapting to Change 96

   Conclusion 99
   References 103

INTRODUCTION

You know that feeling when you're talking to someone, and you can tell they're not even listening? Their eyes are glazed over; they're nodding along, but you know they're mentally checked out. It can be frustrating, right? Well, I've been there too—more times than I'd like to admit.

As an introvert, I've always been a good listener. But here's the thing: being a good listener and being an active listener are two very different things. I had my struggles with really focusing on what people were saying, especially in group settings. My mind wandered, and I'd get lost in my thoughts instead of truly engaging with the conversation.

Over time, I realized that if I wanted to have meaningful relationships and be successful in my career, I needed to step up my listening game. And let me tell you, it's been a journey. From learning to read nonverbal cues to practicing empathy, I've discovered that active listening is a skill that does take time and effort to develop.

And that's precisely what this book is all about. "Stop F*cking Talking and Start Listening: Listen because you might learn something" is your guide to becoming a master listener in all areas of your life. Whether you're struggling to connect with your partner, trying to nail that big presentation at work, or just want to be a better friend, the techniques and strategies in this book will help you level up your listening skills.

Now, what are you thinking: "Listening? That's not exactly a ground-breaking topic." But here's the thing: truly listening has become a rare and valuable skill in a world constantly bombarded with digital distractions and everyone vying for attention. And it's not just about being polite or nodding along—active listening can transform your relationships, your career, and even your sense of self.

Throughout this book, we'll dive into the nitty-gritty of being an active listener. We'll go through the common barriers that get in the way of effective listening, like distractions, biases, and even our own egos. We'll discuss the importance of nonverbal communication and how to read between the lines of what someone's saying. And we'll get practical exercises and real-life scenarios that will help you put your new skills into action.

But this isn't just a dry, academic textbook. We'll also hear from experts in the field, explore the latest research on communication and empathy, and even have a few laughs along the way. Because let's be honest: learning to listen can be challenging, but it doesn't have to be boring.

By the end of this book, you'll have a toolbox full of techniques to help you become a more engaged, empathetic, and effective listener. You'll be able to navigate even the most challenging conversations with grace and understanding. And most importantly, you'll have a deeper appreciation for the power of listening and its impact on every aspect of your life.

So, are you ready to Stop F*cking Talking and Start Listening? Let's dive in.

CHAPTER 1
FOUNDATIONS OF ACTIVE LISTENING

EVER BEEN in a conversation where you felt like the other person was just waiting for you to stop talking so they could start? You know, that awkward moment when you're pouring your heart out, and they're nodding like a bobblehead, eyes glazed over, clearly thinking about their grocery list or what show to binge next. It's not a great feeling, is it? We've all been there, both as the one talking and, if we're honest, as the one zoning out. But here's the kicker: those moments, those tiny blips in our conversations, are precisely why active listening is so important.

Active listening isn't just about catching words—it's about showing up, giving a damn, and genuinely getting what someone's trying to say. And let's face it: In a world where everyone is vying for attention, being a truly good listener is like finding a unicorn. That's why, before we dive into all the nitty-gritty techniques and strategies, we need to lay down some solid foundations. It all starts with empathy.

1.1 THE ART OF EMPATHY IN LISTENING

Empathy is the secret sauce of active listening. It turns a routine conversation into something memorable and meaningful. When you truly empathize, you connect with others on a level deeper than words. You're not just nodding along; you're understanding. Empathy lets you share in someone else's joy, frustration, or excitement, and it's the glue that holds relationships together.

So, how do you build this magical skill? Well, like most things worth doing, it takes practice. Putting yourself in the other person's shoes is the best way to start. Imagine walking their path, seeing the world through their eyes. This perspective-taking isn't just a one-time exercise; it's a mindset shift. You can also try emotional mirroring. Reflect on the feelings you observe, both verbally and non-verbally. It is not about mimicking but genuinely resonating with their emotional state. And because we're all a work in progress, keep a journal to reflect on your interactions. Note moments when you felt truly connected and when you didn't. Over time, you'll start seeing patterns and opportunities for growth.

Empathy isn't just for heart-to-hearts with friends and family. It's a versatile tool that shines in professional settings, too. Picture a workplace where empathy is encouraged. That sounds nice, right? It transforms team dynamics, fosters collaboration, and even boosts productivity. When you empathize with a colleague, you're not just acknowledging their work but valuing their perspective. It can diffuse tension in high-stakes meetings or help you navigate tricky office politics. Similarly, empathy can bridge generational gaps or heal old wounds in family dynamics.

Now, let's talk about the roadblocks. Empathy isn't always easy. We all have biases—those pesky preconceived notions that color our perceptions. They can make it hard to really understand someone else's point of view. To control these, start by acknowledging them. Self-awareness is your friend here. Once you've recognized your biases, you can consciously set them aside. Emotional fatigue is another hurdle. Constantly tuning into others' emotions can be draining. To combat this, ensure you're taking care of yourself. Set boundaries when needed, and give yourself time to recharge.

Empathy Reflection Exercise

Take a moment to reflect on a recent conversation where you felt connected—or disconnected. Jot down the emotions you noticed in yourself and the other person. What helped or hindered your empathy? Consider how you could apply what you've learned to future interactions. You can regularly go back to this exercise to track your progress.

Empathy is more than just a skill; it's a way of being. It's a commitment to understanding and valuing others. As we explore listening further, remember that empathy should be your compass. It will guide you through the complexities of human interaction, ensuring you hear and truly listen.

1.2 BUILDING EMOTIONAL INTELLIGENCE FOR BETTER LISTENING

When listening, we often think about the ears doing all the work. But here's a twist: Our emotional intelligence plays a starring role. Emotional intelligence, or EQ, isn't just some feel-good concept; it's about understanding emotions—yours and others. It's the difference between just hearing words and really "getting" the person behind them. Think of EQ as having a superpower that helps you navigate the emotional landscapes of everyday conversations.

So, what makes up this superpower called EQ? Picture it as a blend of key ingredients: self-awareness, self-regulation, social awareness, and relationship management. Self-awareness is about knowing your own emotional triggers and how they affect your listening. Self-regulation involves checking those emotions so they don't hijack your conversations. Social awareness is tuning into the emotional states of others, much like a human mood ring. Finally, relationship management is about using all the above to build and maintain strong, meaningful connections.

Let's talk strategy. To boost your EQ, start with some good old-fashioned self-awareness exercises. Spend a few minutes each day reflecting on your emotional responses to conversations. What sets you off? What makes you tune out? Once you know your triggers, you can work on self-regulation. Try techniques like deep breathing or counting to ten when emotions are bubbling up. It's like giving your emotions a timeout. Then, move on to social awareness. Practice reading the room by paying attention to body language and tone of voice. It's about noticing what isn't being said. Lastly, hone your relationship management skills. Use positive reinforcement and active listening to enhance your interactions.

EQ isn't just a personal thing; it's a game-changer in real-life scenarios. Imagine you're in a heated debate at work. Instead of reacting impulsively, you pause, recognize your rising frustration, and choose a calm response. That's EQ in action, diffusing tension and fostering collaboration. Or consider a family gathering where emotions run high. With EQ, you can navigate these emotional minefields, turning potential conflicts into opportunities for connection.

Of course, you can't improve what you don't measure, so tracking your EQ growth is crucial. Start with self-assessment tools that gauge your emotional responses and listening habits. Use progress-tracking worksheets to note improvements and setbacks. These tools act like a map, showing where you've been and where you are headed. They help you reflect on your learning curve, reinforcing positive changes while highlighting areas needing more attention.

Emotional intelligence (EQ) in listening is like having a secret weapon. It allows you to connect on a level that goes beyond words. When you develop these skills, you improve your listening and transform how you interact with the world. So, embrace the power of EQ. It's not just about becoming a better listener; it's about becoming a better human. And isn't that what we all want?

1.3 CULTIVATING SELF-AWARENESS THROUGH ACTIVE LISTENING

Imagine sitting in a meeting, nodding along as your colleague presents a new idea. Your mind, however, is a million miles away, pondering whether you left the iron on or what to have for dinner. Sound familiar? We've all been there. But here's the thing: self-awareness in listening is like a mental spotlight that helps us recognize when we're drifting and pull ourselves back into the moment. It's the secret ingredient that turns passive hearing into active engagement. When we become aware of our listening habits, we can identify patterns, biases, and triggers that keep us from truly understanding others. This self-awareness is crucial because recognizing these habits is the first step toward transforming them.

Now, let's get practical. Developing self-awareness is all about taking a good, hard look in the mirror—not literally, unless you're into that, in which case, go wild. Start by reflecting on your listening experiences. After a conversation, ask yourself: Was I truly present? What emotions surfaced, and how did they impact my listening? This self-reflection is like a mental inventory that helps you pinpoint areas for improvement. Another powerful tool is feedback from peers and mentors. Sure, it stings a little to hear that you zone out during meetings, but constructive criticism is a goldmine for growth. When someone points out a listening hiccup, don't get defensive. Instead, view it as an opportunity to improve your skills.

Mindfulness practices are also game-changers for self-awareness. Engage in mindfulness meditation exercises that train your brain to focus on the present moment. Just like how you wouldn't scroll through Instagram during a yoga class, try not to let your mind wander during conversations. Practicing mindfulness regularly helps train your mind to stay present, making it easier to manage distracting thoughts. Like any positive habit, it takes consistency to see results. Set aside a bit of time each day—whether it's a few minutes of stillness or just paying attention to your breath—to build this helpful routine.

But let's not forget about those sneaky listening biases. We all have preconceived notions and assumptions that color our understanding. It's like wearing sunglasses indoors; they distort the view. Recognizing cognitive biases involves acknowledging that they're there in the first place. Once you do, you can actively work to neutralize them. For instance, if you tend to dismiss ideas from certain people, remind yourself to approach each conversation with an open mind. One strategy is actively challenging your assumptions by asking questions and seeking clarification. This will enhance your understanding and show others that you're genuinely invested in what they have to say.

So, why does all this self-awareness stuff matter? Because it paves the way for more effective communication. When you know your tendencies, you can adjust your listening style to better connect with others. Picture this: You're in a heated debate, and instead of reacting defensively, you pause, recognize your emotional triggers, and respond thoughtfully. This level of awareness transforms conflict into constructive dialogue. The ripple effect extends beyond individual interactions, too. Self-aware listening can lead to stronger teamwork, improved problem-solving, and even career advancement in professional settings. And in personal relationships, it fosters deeper connections and mutual respect.

Ultimately, self-awareness is the bridge to understanding others and ourselves more clearly.

1.4 THE ROLE OF MINDFULNESS IN ENHANCING LISTENING

Mindful listening. Sounds kinda zen, right? But before you picture yourself sitting cross-legged in a room filled with incense, let's break it down. Mindful listening is about being fully present, truly soaking in the conversation without letting your mind wander off to what's for dinner or that email you forgot to send. It's like giving the speaker a mental hug, letting them know you're there with them. The benefits? They're pretty fantastic. You become more engaged and pick up on the nuances in conversations, and, most importantly, the speaker feels genuinely heard. When you're mindful, you're not just waiting for your turn to talk. You're engaged, focused, and connected.

So, how do you get there without turning into a meditation guru? It starts with simple practices that return you to the here and now. Breathing exercises are an underrated gem. Next time you're in a chat, try this: Take a slow, deep breath, and let it out gently. This act alone can center you, making it easier to focus on what's being said. Think of it as hitting the reset button on your brain. Then, there's the power of observation. Pay attention to non-verbal cues—the way someone's eyes crinkle when they smile or their slight frown when they're confused. These little details tell you as much as words do. Try a listening meditation session if you're looking for something more structured. It's about dedicating time just to listen to the sounds around you or a guided meditation track. It trains your brain to register more than just surface-level noise.

Bringing mindfulness into everyday interactions doesn't mean you must overhaul your routine. Start small. In conversations, remind yourself to be present. If you catch your mind drifting, don't beat yourself up. Gently guide your focus back; lightly pinch the inside of your wrist when your spacing out can be a simple cue for yourself. Over time, these little habits become second nature. A fun tip is to treat each conversation like a mystery novel. Hang onto every word, anticipate twists, and try to predict where the conversation might lead. It keeps your brain engaged and curious.

Distractions are the arch-nemeses of listening. Distractions are everywhere, from the ping of your phone to that stray thought about what's in the fridge. But with mindfulness, you can tackle them head-on. Start by creating a distraction-free zone when you're in meaningful conversations. Mute your phone, close unnecessary tabs on your computer, and position yourself away from bustling areas. It's like creating a mini fortress of concentration. To manage interruptions, practice the art of polite boundaries. If someone interrupts, acknowledge them but steer the conversation back to the speaker. It's about maintaining the flow without being dismissive.

For sustained attention, try the "5-4-3-2-1" technique. It's a grounding exercise in which you identify five things you see, four things you hear, three things you can touch, two things you can smell, and one thing you can taste. This exercise draws you into the present and clears the mental cobwebs. Remember, mindfulness isn't about achieving a constant state of zen. It's about repeatedly returning to the moment, like returning to a favorite book you can't put down.

Mindful listening might sound simple, but its impact is profound. It transforms how you interact with the world. You're not just hearing;

you're experiencing conversations. And in a world filled with noise, that's a powerful skill to have.

1.5 CREATING TRUST WITH EVERY CONVERSATION

Picture this: You're at a dinner party, and someone leans in during the conversation, genuinely interested in your story. Their attention is unwavering, their responses thoughtful, and you can't help but feel valued. That's trust at work. It's the bedrock of effective communication, creating a space where open and honest dialogue can grow. In the world of listening, trust isn't just a nice-to-have thing; it's the glue that holds everything together. When we trust that our words are received sincerely, we're more likely to open up and share what's truly on our minds. This bond is what makes communication meaningful and memorable.

Trust in listening isn't just about nodding along politely. It's about showing up consistently, proving that you're reliable and that your words align with your actions. Think of it as building a bridge, one conversation at a time. Consistency and reliability both play starring roles here. You demonstrate that you're dependable when you show up for conversations regularly, whether it's a morning meeting or a late-night chat. Active listening confirmations—like little nods, verbal affirmations, and thoughtful questions—also demonstrate your engagement and involvement. And let's not forget the power of genuine interest. When you show curiosity about the person you're conversing with, it creates a bond that's hard to break.

But what happens when trust takes a hit? You may have missed a crucial detail in a conversation, or you were distracted, and the other person noticed. It happens to the best of us. Repairing trust is a delicate thing, but it's entirely possible. Start with a sincere apology. Acknowledge the misstep without making excuses, and take responsibility for your actions. Accountability is key. Next, engage in trust-building exercises. Establish new communication rituals, like regular check-ins or setting aside distraction-free time, to show you're committed to improvement. Repairing trust isn't about sweeping things under the rug but showing you're willing to make things right.

Trust-building isn't a one-size-fits-all endeavor. It requires adaptation to different contexts. Trust involves spending quality time together in family settings, listening without judgment, and being there when it matters most. Family trust-building activities, like game nights or shared projects, can reinforce bonds and create lasting memories. On the professional front, trust might mean delivering what you promise, respecting confidentiality, and actively contributing to a collaborative environment. In both cases, the goal is to create areas where people feel safe to express themselves and be heard.

Trust-Building Checklist

For Family:

- Schedule regular family gatherings or activities.
- Practice active listening during family discussions.
- Create a safe space for open communication.

For Work:

- Deliver on promises and deadlines consistently.
- Respect confidentiality and privacy.
- Encourage open dialogue in team meetings.

As we wrap up this section, remember that trust isn't built overnight. It's a continuous process requiring patience and dedication, but the rewards are worth it. When trust is present, conversations become more than just exchanges of words; they become connections that enrich our lives. So, as you navigate the listening world, keep trust at the forefront. Embrace it and watch as it transforms your interactions into something extraordinary.

CHAPTER 2
OVERCOMING LISTENING BARRIERS

IMAGINE THIS: you're at a family gathering, and Uncle Joe is again going on about his theory that Elvis is alive and well, living as a barista in Grand Rapids. As you nod along, your mind starts to wander. You might be tempted to dismiss him outright, but hold up! This is where we need to talk about those sneaky biases that can derail our listening. Biases are like those uninvited guests who show up at your mental party, making a mess of things. They creep in unannounced and skew your perception before you even get a chance to process what's being said. So, let's look at these biases and figure out how to show them the door.

First up, we have confirmation bias. This one's a real doozy. It's like having a personal cheerleader in your head who only roots for the ideas you already believe in. When you're stuck in confirmation bias, you're more likely to tune into information that supports your beliefs and ignore anything that contradicts them. So, when Uncle Joe insists on his Elvis tale, your confirmation bias might nudge you to agree just because it's easier than challenging him. Then there's stereotyping, like putting people into boxes marked "Handle with Prejudice." It simplifies complex human beings into flat, one-dimensional characters. When you stereotype, you miss out on the rich tapestry of experiences and perspectives others bring.

Recognizing these biases is the first step to kicking them to the curb. Self-reflection is your new best friend here. Think about keeping a journal where you jot down instances when your biases might have clouded your judgment. Did you jump to conclusions about a coworker's idea because you don't see eye to eye on other matters? Did you dismiss a friend's advice because it didn't fit your narrative? A worksheet can be handy for this: list biases, examples when they popped up, and how they affected your interactions. Self-awareness is a key player in this game.

To tackle these biases, we need some strategies. Think about perspective-taking as putting on someone else's glasses for a moment. It might not correct your vision, but at least you'll see things from their point of view. When Uncle Joe talks about Elvis, instead of rolling your eyes, imagine why he might hold onto that belief. Maybe it's a nostalgic connection to his youth. Perspective-taking exercises, such as role-playing scenarios in which you argue from the other person's viewpoint, can be surprisingly effective. They open up pathways in your brain that you didn't even know existed.

Another strategy is fostering open-mindedness. Picture your mind as a house with all the windows and doors flung wide open. It's about letting in fresh air and new ideas. Try an exercise where you actively seek out opinions you disagree with. Listen to a podcast from the opposite political spectrum or read an article that challenges your views. The goal isn't to change your beliefs overnight but to learn how to entertain diverse perspectives without immediately rejecting them.

Creating a bias-free environment is no small feat, but it's not impossible, either. Group settings can be breeding grounds for biases, especially when everyone tends to nod in agreement just to keep the peace. To counter this, encourage inclusivity by inviting quieter voices to share their thoughts. Use strategies like rotating facilitators in meetings to ensure that no single perspective dominates. When everyone feels heard and respected, biases have less room to maneuver.

Bias-Checking Exercise

Take a moment to reflect on a recent conversation where you felt your biases might have influenced your listening. Ask yourself: What assumptions did I make? How did those assumptions impact my understanding? Write down one action you can take to challenge this bias in future interactions.

Remember, biases aren't bad guys lurking in the shadows. They're just shortcuts our brains take to make sense of the world. But, like any shortcut, they can lead us astray. The real goal is to become aware of them, acknowledge their influence, and work toward minimizing their impact on our listening.

2.1 MANAGING EMOTIONAL REACTIONS FOR CLEARER COMMUNICATION

Picture this: You're in the middle of a conversation, and suddenly, something hits a nerve. Your heart rate spikes, your palms get sweaty, and before you know it, words you didn't mean to say are spilling out. Emotional triggers are those sneaky little landmines that can explode into our conversations without warning. They come in all shapes and sizes, from a well-meaning but ill-timed comment from a friend to how your boss phrases feedback. The key is to spot them before they control the narrative. It could be the tone of voice that reminds you of past criticisms or the topic that stirs up old feelings. Recognizing these triggers is like knowing where the potholes are on your usual route—once you know them, you can navigate them more smoothly.

Now, let's talk about emotional regulation. Imagine your emotions as a wild horse galloping in every direction. Emotional regulation is your trusty lasso, bringing those feelings under control. A reliable go-to technique is deep breathing. It might seem basic—even a bit too easy— but pausing so you can take a few deep breaths can make a big difference. Slowly inhale through your nose, then hold it for a few seconds, and exhale through your mouth. It's like hitting the pause button on your emotional response, giving you a moment to think before you react. Then, there's cognitive reframing, which is giving your thoughts a makeover. When faced with a triggering comment, instead of spiraling, ask yourself: Is there another way to interpret this? Could it be a misunderstanding or a different perspective? This shift in thinking can defuse emotional reactions and lead to clearer communication.

Staying composed in heated situations is easier said than done, right? But with a few strategies in your pocket, it becomes more manageable. Practice calming techniques like visualization. Before entering a high-stress discussion, picture a place where you feel at ease—maybe a beach or a quiet park. Let this image anchor you when things get tense. Another strategy is role-playing. It might sound theatrical, but practicing difficult conversations with a friend can prepare you for the real thing. It's like a dress rehearsal for your emotions, allowing you to explore responses in a safe environment.

Building emotional resilience requires consistent effort and practice, kind of like training for a marathon. Start by incorporating resilience-building activities into your daily routine. Consider journaling about your emotional experiences—what triggered you, how you reacted, and what you learned. Over time, this reflection can help you identify patterns and build a toolkit for handling emotions. Mindfulness exercises like short meditation sessions can also strengthen your emotional resilience. These techniques help you stay grounded in the moment, making it less likely you'll be overwhelmed by emotions and more likely to respond thoughtfully instead of reacting impulsively.

Emotional resilience is about bouncing back from emotional triggers and life's ups and downs. It's about building a state of mind where challenges are opportunities for growth and not obstacles. And while it won't make emotions disappear, it will set you up with the skills to manage them more effectively. So, the next time you're in a conversation with someone and feel those familiar emotions bubbling up, you'll be ready, armed with the skills to keep your cool and communicate clearly.

2.2 FOCUS AND PRESENCE: THE ART OF STAYING ENGAGED

Sitting in a meeting, you might find your mind drifting to what you're having for dinner or wondering if you locked the front door. We've all been there. But staying focused is crucial for effective listening and understanding. Think of focus as the glue that holds the pieces of a conversation together. When you're truly focused, you're not just hearing words; you're connecting the dots, picking up on nuances, and actually understanding what's being said. This connection is what transforms a conversation from a mere exchange of words into a meaningful dialogue.

So, how do you boost your focus when the world is full of distractions? Start with active listening cues. These are like little mental post-it notes reminding you to stay present. Simple things like nodding, maintaining eye contact, and providing verbal affirmations can keep you engaged. They signal to the other person that you're there with them, not off somewhere in la-la land. Next, try incorporating mental note-taking methods. This doesn't mean scribbling down every word; instead, focus on capturing key points or interesting ideas. Mentally summarizing what's being said helps you stay in the moment and enhances your comprehension.

But let's be real—maintaining focus over time is no small feat. It's like running a marathon. You need endurance. Try exercises that build conversational stamina, like setting a timer and practicing focused listening for short bursts. Gradually increase the time as your focus improves. Another handy tool is monitoring your engagement levels. As soon as you notice that your mind may be starting to wander, you slowly bring it back. Think of it as steering a car back on track after veering slightly off course. This self-awareness is key to staying engaged, even in long or complex discussions.

Now, we can't ignore those pesky internal distractions. You know, the ones where your brain starts crafting grocery lists or daydreaming about your next vacation. Managing wandering thoughts is a skill worth developing. Start by acknowledging the thought and then gently redirecting your focus. Picture your thoughts as clouds passing by. You don't have to engage with every one of them. Another technique is to practice single-tasking. In a world that glorifies multitasking, there's power in giving your full attention to one thing at a time. When you're listening, just listen. Don't try to solve world hunger; remember your Netflix password simultaneously.

Internal distractions also love to team up with multitasking, turning your brain into a chaotic circus. Taming this chaos requires discipline. Begin by recognizing when you're multitasking. Maybe you're checking emails while someone's talking. Pause, set aside the distraction, and return to the conversation. Use mindfulness techniques to anchor yourself in the present. A simple breathing exercise or a quick scan of your surroundings can ground you, bringing your attention back to the conversation at hand. Remember, the goal is to be present, not perfect.

Focus and presence aren't just about being physically present; they're about genuinely engaging with the person in front of you and making them feel heard and valued. When you prioritize focus, you're opening the door to deeper understanding and richer interactions.

2.3 BREAKING DOWN CULTURAL BARRIERS IN LISTENING

Ever find yourself in a conversation where you're nodding along, but deep down, you know there's a disconnect? Often, this gap stems from cultural differences that influence how we communicate. Culture shapes not just what we say but how we say it and even what we choose not to say. In some cultures, silence is golden, a sign of respect or contemplation, while in others, it might be seen as awkward or even rude. Then there's the matter of directness. People get straight to the point in some places; no beating around the bush. In others, indirect communication is the norm—saving face and maintaining harmony take center stage. It's like being handed a puzzle with a few missing pieces; you know the picture is there, but you're not quite seeing it yet. If you want to be a better listener and not come off as clueless in cross-cultural conversations, paying attention to these details is a must.

Consider diving into cultural sensitivity training to navigate these cultural waters. Think of it as a crash course in global communication etiquette. These sessions often involve role-playing exercises where you get to practice different communication styles. It's like stretching before a workout; it prepares you for the real thing. Another effective approach is active cultural learning, which involves immersing yourself in the cultural practices of others. It doesn't take much—go to a cultural event, try food you can't pronounce, or have a real conversation with someone outside your usual circle. The more you expose yourself to diverse perspectives, the more those cultural barriers crumble. It's about opening your mind to a world of possibilities and seeing things from angles you hadn't considered before.

Building cultural awareness is like discovering a new dimension in your conversations. It's not just about recognizing differences but truly appreciating them. A great way to increase your cultural awareness is through workshops focusing on understanding cultural norms and practices. These workshops often include activities like storytelling, where participants share their cultural experiences and traditions. It's a chance to hear firsthand how culture shapes communication and to see the world through someone else's eyes. The goal is to move beyond stereotypes and assumptions and toward a richer understanding of the diverse tapestry of human interaction. Think of a black-and-white sketch that has color added to it; suddenly, everything is more vivid and nuanced.

Now, let's talk about applying this cultural knowledge in real conversations. Imagine you're working on a project with a team that's as diverse as a United Nations gathering. Each member brings their own cultural lens to the table, which can either be a recipe for chaos or a symphony of collaboration. When you apply cultural understanding, you become the conductor, guiding the orchestra to create harmony. Case studies of successful cross-cultural interactions often highlight the importance of active listening and patience. Take, for example, a multinational team working on a marketing campaign. The team members took the time to understand each other's cultural contexts, leading to a campaign that resonated with a global audience. By valuing each person's input and adapting to different communication styles, they turned potential barriers into bridges of understanding.

In our interconnected world, breaking down cultural barriers isn't just a nice-to-have skill; it's a necessity. It's about honoring the rich diversity that surrounds us and using it to enrich our interactions. Understanding cultural differences, engaging in active learning, building awareness, and applying this knowledge in conversations can turn potential pitfalls into opportunities for deeper connections. It's about becoming a cultural chameleon, adapting and thriving in any environment, and at the end of the day, isn't that what being a great listener is all about?

2.4 NAVIGATING LISTENING BLOCKS AND DISTRACTIONS

Ever find yourself nodding along in a conversation, only to realize you have no idea what the other person just said? You're not alone. Listening blocks are common culprits that stand in the way of genuine communication. These blocks come in many forms, like assumptions and preoccupations. Assumptions are those pesky mental shortcuts where we think we know what the other person will say, so we tune out. Meanwhile, preoccupations are like mental hijackers, pulling our attention away with thoughts of unfinished tasks, looming deadlines, or even what we're having for dinner. These barriers can pop up in everyday situations, like when you're trying to listen to your partner vent about their day while your mind drafts tomorrow's to-do list.

Distractions are like the confetti of the listening world—colorful, numerous, and sometimes unavoidable. But there are ways to minimize their impact. One effective strategy is creating a conducive environment. Think of your ideal listening space as a sanctuary from the chaos. It might mean turning off your phone, stepping away from your computer, or simply choosing a quieter room. This space becomes a bubble of focus, free from the digital and physical noise that often competes for our attention. Alongside this, focusing techniques can work wonders. These might include visualization exercises, where you imagine your mind as a clear, still pond, with each ripple representing new information. This imagery can help center your thoughts and bring your attention to the conversation.

Focusing on the task at hand can also benefit from specific exercises. Consider attention-building drills, which are like gym workouts for your mind. Start with short, focused listening sessions, gradually increasing the duration as your mental stamina grows. It's similar to building endurance for a marathon, but thankfully, without the blisters. Techniques to quickly regain focus can be your lifeline in a conversation. If you notice your mind wandering, try a quick mental count or a shift in posture. These small adjustments can serve as a reset button, anchoring you back at the moment and ensuring you don't miss out on important details.

Creating a distraction-resistant mindset is about more than just quick fixes; it's about building a mental fortress that can withstand the barrage of everyday interruptions. Mindset development activities can help strengthen this fortress. Start with mindfulness practices, which can train your mind to recognize distractions as they arise and gently guide your attention back. Think of it like herding a flock of sheep—your thoughts are the sheep, and mindfulness is the shepherd, bringing them back whenever they wander too far. Don't try to power through the whole day—take a few breathers so your brain doesn't tap out by lunchtime.

As we wrap up this chapter, consider how these skills fit into the bigger picture. Effective Listening isn't just about hearing—it's about actually giving a sh*t and making a real connection. Addressing listening blocks and distractions opens the door to more meaningful interactions. These skills improve conversations, enhance relationships, foster empathy, and build trust. Next, we'll explore how these listening foundations can be put into practice, turning theory into action and enriching our lives in unexpected ways.

CHAPTER 3
NONVERBAL COMMUNICATION MASTERY

PICTURE THIS: you're at a party, and across the room, someone waves. You wave back, but wait—were they waving at you or the person behind you? Awkward, right? Ah, the wonders of body language. It's that silent communicator, always at work whether you know it or not. Our bodies constantly send signals—sometimes loud, sometimes subtle—that speak volumes about our emotions and intentions. From how you stand to the tilt of your head, these nonverbal cues make up a substantial part of how we interact. Body language is so powerful that it often overshadows the words we use. It's like that sidekick in a superhero movie who ends up stealing the show.

So, let's get down to basics. Body language encompasses gestures, posture, facial expressions, and eye contact. It's everything your body does to communicate without uttering a single word. Think of it as a secret language everyone speaks but few truly understand. Common signals include crossed arms, which might scream "stay away," or a genuine smile that invites you in. And those small nods during a conversation? They're like little breadcrumbs leading the way to engagement. The impact of these cues is profound. They can reinforce your message or completely contradict it. Imagine saying, "I'm fine," while you have your arms crossed and you're avoiding eye contact.

Not very convincing, is it? That's the magic—and sometimes the mischief—of body language.

Now, you might be wondering how to read this cryptic language effectively. Start by observing congruence. This means checking if someone's verbal and nonverbal messages align. If a friend insists they're okay but their shoulders are slumped and their eyes are downcast, their body might tell a different story. Pay attention to clusters of signals rather than isolated actions. A single gesture can be misleading, but a group of consistent cues can offer a clearer picture. For practice, try a simple exercise: watch a TV show on mute and see how much of the plot you can follow just by observing body language. It's like a detective game with less risk of getting caught in a rain-soaked alley.

Body language isn't just something you interpret; it's also something you project. Consciously using body language can enhance your listening and communication skills. Start with an open posture. This means facing the person you're talking to with your arms relaxed and shoulders back. It conveys interest and approachability. Eye contact is another powerful tool. It signals engagement and confidence, but remember, there's a fine line between attentive and creepy. Think of eye contact as a gentle dance, not a staring contest. And don't forget those nods and verbal affirmations—they're the unsung heroes of active listening, reassuring the speaker that you're with them all the way.

But beware, interpreting body language isn't an exact science. Misinterpretations happen, sometimes because of cultural differences. For example, direct eye contact is considered confident in many Western cultures but might be considered confrontational in some Asian or Middle Eastern cultures. It's like playing a game of telephone with gestures, where meanings can get lost in translation. To avoid these pitfalls, approach body language interpretation with an open mind and a dash of humility. If you're unsure, ask for clarification. It's better to seek understanding than to assume and risk miscommunication.

Body Language Reflection Exercise

Take a moment to reflect on a recent interaction. Consider the body language cues you noticed. Did they align with the spoken words? Write down any discrepancies and consider how they influenced your understanding of the conversation. Try this exercise regularly to hone your interpretive skills.

Body language is a fascinating communication element, offering a window into the unspoken thoughts and feelings of those around us. Once you get the hang of reading these signals, your conversations will improve dramatically, and your connections will feel a lot more real.

3.1 FACIAL EXPRESSIONS: READING BETWEEN THE LINES

Facial expressions are like an emotional billboard. They advertise what's going on inside without needing a single word. Think about it: A smile can light up a room, while a frown can cast a shadow over even the sunniest day. These expressions are universal emotional indicators that cut across languages and cultures. A genuine smile, known by the crinkling at the corners of the eyes, signals happiness. A furrowed brow and downturned lips convey sadness or concern. Even a quick eye roll can speak volumes about someone's annoyance or sarcasm without them saying anything. Facial expressions are powerful because they offer a direct line to someone's emotional state, often more honestly than words do.

Accurately interpreting these facial cues, however, requires a bit of practice. It's not just about recognizing the obvious expressions like a smile or a frown. It's about picking up on those fleeting micro-expressions that flash across someone's face in a split second. These tiny movements are like emotional breadcrumbs, hinting at feelings that might not be fully expressed verbally. Start by honing your skills through micro-expression recognition practice. Look for quick changes in someone's expression—like a flash of surprise or a momentary downcast eye. These can reveal underlying emotions that aren't openly shared. Engaging in facial expression analysis exercises can sharpen your skills. Watch a silent film or mute a TV show and focus solely on interpreting the characters' emotions through their expressions. It's a fun way to train your brain to spot the subtle shifts in facial cues.

But here's where it gets interesting—cultural differences can make interpreting facial expressions a bit like solving a mystery. What might be a friendly gesture in one culture could be misread as something entirely different in another. For instance, a smile showing teeth is often seen as genuine in Western cultures, yet in some Asian cultures, a closed-mouth smile is considered more polite. Understanding these cultural variations is crucial for avoiding misunderstandings in cross-cultural interactions. It's like being a detective, piecing together clues to understand the whole story. Being aware of these nuances can prevent you from jumping to conclusions based solely on your cultural lens.

Incorporating facial expression analysis into your listening practice can elevate your communication skills. If you actually pay attention to the cues, people tell you how they feel—even when their words don't. Take, for example, a case study in which a manager noticed that despite his employee's verbal agreement in meetings, her concerned expressions told a different story. Recognizing this discrepancy, he approached her privately, leading to a valuable discussion where she shared her genuine concerns about the project. This awareness allowed the manager to address potential issues before they became major problems. Facial expressions enhance our grasp of spoken language by providing extra context, helping us better interpret the overall message.

Incorporating the analysis of facial cues into your active listening is like adding an extra channel of communication. It's not just about hearing what's said but also about seeing what's felt. This skill can transform your interactions, making them richer and more meaningful. Whether in personal or professional settings, understanding and interpreting facial expressions can bridge gaps, defuse tension, and build stronger connections. In a world where so much is said without words, being able to read between the lines is a game-changer.

3.2 UNDERSTANDING GESTURES ACROSS CULTURES

Gestures are like the emojis of the real world—they add flavor to our conversations and help convey meaning beyond words. They're the subtle nods, waves, and hand flicks that punctuate our interactions, making them more vibrant and engaging. But these little movements aren't just random; they carry specific meanings that can vary widely depending on where you are. For instance, a thumbs-up might seem like a universal sign for "good job," but in some cultures, it means something else entirely. It can be considered offensive in some parts of the Middle East. The classic peace sign, when flipped around, turns from a symbol of harmony to an insult in places like the UK. It's fascinating but also a little daunting—navigating the world of gestures requires both awareness and a touch of cultural sensitivity.

The cultural kaleidoscope doesn't stop there. Take the simple act of pointing with your index finger. In some cultures, it's as common as breathing. But in others, like in Malaysia or the Philippines, it can come across as impolite or even aggressive. Instead, they might use their entire hand or a nod to direct attention. Cultural norms and historical contexts can heavily influence the interpretation of gestures. In Japan, bowing is seen as a gesture of respect, and how deep the bow is indicates the level of respect or gratitude. Meanwhile, an open palm gesture, known as "moutza," is an ancient insult in Greece. These differences can be fascinating and confusing, leading to misinterpretations if you're not careful.

So, how do you use gestures effectively when interacting with people from different cultures? Start by doing a little homework. Understanding the cultural context of the people you're engaging with can save you from a lot of awkward moments. If traveling or working with international colleagues, familiarize yourself with their customs and common gestures. But don't worry; you don't need to become a walking encyclopedia of gestures. Simple strategies can go a long way. When in doubt, observe more and gesture less. Watch how locals use their hands and mimic their style if it feels appropriate. If you're unsure about a gesture's meaning, it's perfectly okay to ask. This displays respect and your willingness to learn, which can go a long way in building rapport.

Exercises in cross-cultural gesture use can be both enlightening and fun. Try hosting a gesture swap with friends from different backgrounds. Share gestures from your culture and learn theirs in return. It's like a cultural exchange program focused on hand signals. Not only will you pick up on the nuances of different gestures, but you'll also gain insights into the cultures behind them. Practicing this skill helps you adjust your gestures to fit your audience, leading to more effective and culturally aware communication.

Clarity is key to avoiding gesture miscommunication. If a gesture seems to cause confusion, follow it up with verbal clarification. It's like adding subtitles to a foreign film. You get the gist from the visuals, but the words fill in the blanks. Also, be mindful of your surroundings. In formal settings, it's usually safer to keep gestures to a minimum unless you know their appropriateness. In more relaxed environments, feel free to use gestures, but keep an eye on the reactions of those around you. If someone seems puzzled, it might be time to switch gears.

Gestures are a powerful tool in the communication toolkit, offering a rich layer of meaning beyond spoken language. But with great power comes great responsibility. Awareness of and adapting to cultural differences in gestures can prevent misunderstandings and foster stronger connections across diverse groups.

3.3 POSTURE AND PROXIMITY: UNSPOKEN ELEMENTS OF INTERACTION

Just imagine yourself in front of a crowd, ready to deliver a killer presentation. You stand tall, shoulders back and chest open. You feel confident, and you look it, too. That's the power of posture. It doesn't just influence how others see you; it changes how you see yourself. An open and relaxed posture suggests you're approachable and confident. Compare that to crossing your arms and hunching your shoulders— suddenly, you seem defensive or closed off. This simple change can affect how your message is perceived. It's like switching from a low-quality selfie to a professional headshot; the impact is immediate and significant. People tend to perceive you as more authoritative and credible when you stand tall and open, which can be a game-changer in personal and professional settings.

Now, let's talk about proximity. You know that feeling when someone stands a little too close, and you instinctively step back? That's the magic of personal space at work. Proximity can forge bonds or create barriers, depending on how you handle it. In a cozy setting with friends, being close can signal intimacy and trust. But in a business meeting, you might want more space to maintain professionalism. Understanding the appropriate distance in various contexts is crucial. It's not just about where you stand; it's about knowing when to step forward and when to hang back. In some cultures, close proximity is a sign of warmth and friendliness, while in others, it might be considered intrusive.

Adjusting both your posture and proximity can enhance your listening skills. Start by being mindful of your posture when you're in a conversation. Lean slightly forward to show you're engaged, but avoid invading the other person's space. It's a delicate balance, like walking a tightrope. Practice exercises that help you become more aware of your space bubble. Stand in different positions and ask a trusted friend for feedback on how your posture and distance feel. You'll be surprised at how these small adjustments can make a big difference in how you're perceived and how effectively you listen.

With all this talk of space, it's important to remember that everyone has different comfort zones. It's like each person has an invisible hula hoop around them that dictates how close you can get. Respecting these boundaries is vital, especially when considering cultural differences. Some folks might prefer a handshake, while others go in for a hug. Boundary awareness isn't just about avoiding awkward situations —it's about showing respect and understanding. Being attuned to these unspoken rules allows you to navigate interactions smoothly and make others feel at ease.

Boundary-setting practices can help you gauge and respect personal space. One method is to watch for subtle cues like a person stepping back or leaning away. These are signs that you might be encroaching on their comfort zone. If you're unsure, don't hesitate to ask. It might feel awkward at first, but a simple "Is this okay?" can go a long way. Customizing your approach based on the context and the individuals involved will make your interactions more fluid and comfortable for everyone involved.

3.4 ENHANCING DIGITAL COMMUNICATION WITH NONVERBAL CUES

When you're chatting digitally or online, you miss out on all the little stuff—smiles, nods, eye rolls—that usually help you read the vibe of a conversation. In digital settings, these cues are often lost or misinterpreted, leading to misunderstandings that can make even the most straightforward messages feel like a game of charades. For instance, a delayed response can be taken as disinterest, while in reality, it's just someone stepping away to make a coffee. Without the physical presence, our usual communication tools are limited, making it harder to gauge emotions or intentions. It's like trying to dance without music—you can do it, but it's not the same.

But don't despair. There are ways to bridge this gap and bring some nonverbal cues into our digital interactions. One simple yet effective tool is the use of emojis and reactions. They might seem trivial, but a well-placed smiley face or thumbs-up can convey warmth and approval, much like a nod or a grin in person. It's like adding salt to a dish—it enhances the flavor and makes the conversation more palatable. Then, there's video call etiquette. Sure, you can't high-five someone through the screen, but maintaining eye contact with the camera instead of looking at your own image can mimic eye contact. It makes the other person feel seen, even if it's through pixels. And remember, your surroundings matter, too. Having a cluttered or flashy background can distract from your message, while a tidy, professional setting conveys focus and attention.

Reading nonverbal signals in virtual environments requires a bit of finesse. The tone of voice can tell you a lot about how someone feels. A flat tone might suggest boredom or irritation, while a lively one indicates enthusiasm. Listen for changes in pitch and pace; they're the digital equivalent of body language. Visual cues, though limited on a screen, are still valuable. Watch for facial expressions and hand movements during video calls. A raised eyebrow or a relaxed posture can give clues about the speaker's mood or level of comfort. It's like being a detective, piecing together clues to form a complete picture.

Keeping engagement high in digital communication can be a challenge. Without the physical presence, attention spans can wander faster than you can say "Zoom fatigue." One way to combat this is by ensuring you're making eye contact. This means looking at the camera rather than the screen on video calls. Initially, it might feel awkward, but it gives the impression that you're fully focused on the conversation. In virtual settings, asking open-ended questions is the online version of making eye contact—it shows you're engaged and encourages others to join the conversation.

While digital communication has limitations, it also offers plenty of opportunities for those open to adapting. With the right adjustments and a touch of creativity, you can make your online interactions feel more personal and engaging. It's about finding new ways to connect, even when physical proximity isn't an option. As we continue to explore the world of listening, keep these digital strategies in mind. They're not just about making your point—they're about ensuring your message is heard, understood, and felt.

CHAPTER 4
PRACTICAL EXERCISES FOR LISTENING IMPROVEMENT

EVER BEEN in a conversation and suddenly realized your brain is playing a highlight reel of last night's dreams instead of processing the words coming out of your friend's mouth? You're not alone. Our minds love to wander, especially when we're supposed to be focused. But what if I told you there's a way to hit the mental pause button and bring yourself back to the here and now? Enter mindfulness—a simple yet powerful tool that can transform your listening skills from average to extraordinary. Mindfulness is about being fully present and experiencing the moment without judgment, and it's a game-changer for active listening. It's like taking your brain to the gym, building those mental muscles to keep distractions at bay.

Mindfulness is rooted in principles that can push us to live in the present. It's about tuning into the now, letting go of the past and future, and engaging with what's directly in front of us. This practice enhances listening by sharpening focus and fostering presence. When you're mindful, you're not just hearing words; you're absorbing the essence of the conversation. Mindful listening involves giving someone your undivided attention, making them feel valued and heard. Philosopher Martin Heidegger identified listening as the key to maintaining meaningful relationships. It's like turning up the volume on empathy and turning down the noise of your internal chatter.

The foundation of mindfulness in listening starts with mindful breathing exercises. Breathing is something we do all day, every day, but rarely with intention. Want to get centered before a chat? Just take a deep breath, hold it for a bit, and let it out nice and slow. This isn't just about oxygen; it's about centering yourself and preparing to be present. Select a relaxing area, free from distractions, where you can focus on your breathing. Think of it as a warm-up routine for your brain before diving into a conversation. This practice helps clear the mental fog and preps you for active listening.

Mindful observation is another powerful tool. It involves being fully present in conversations and paying attention to verbal and nonverbal cues. Imagine sitting in a café, listening to a friend share a funny story. Instead of letting your mind wander all over the place, focus on their words, tone, and body language. Notice how their eyes light up with excitement or how their hands gesture animatedly. These cues add depth to the narrative, making the conversation richer and more engaging. By practicing mindful observation, you're not just hearing the story; you're experiencing it with all your senses.

Using mindfulness throughout your day doesn't require a complete lifestyle overhaul. Start small, with mindfulness reminders sprinkled throughout your day. Set a gentle alarm or use sticky notes as cues to pause, take a breath, and refocus. Whether at work, home, or out and about, these reminders can help you maintain mindfulness and improve your listening skills over time. Developing a personal mindfulness plan tailored to your lifestyle can also make a world of difference. It's about finding what works for you- a morning meditation session, a quiet moment with a cup of tea, or a mindful walk in the park. These practices anchor you in the present, enhancing your ability to listen actively.

Mindful Listening Checklist

- Pause and Breathe: Before starting a conversation, take three deep breaths to center yourself.
- Engage Your Senses: Focus on the speaker's tone, expressions, and gestures.

- Use Mindful Reminders: Set reminders to practice mindfulness throughout the day.
- Reflect on Conversations: After a conversation, take a moment to consider what you learned and how you listened.

Integrating mindfulness into your listening routine is like giving your conversations a turbo boost. It elevates your interactions, making them more meaningful and rewarding for you and the people you engage with.

4.1 EMPATHY-BUILDING ACTIVITIES FOR PERSONAL GROWTH

Have you ever watched a scene in a movie and felt so connected to the character that you couldn't help but feel their joy or pain? That's empathy in action and a powerful tool for personal growth. One way to nurture this skill is through role-playing exercises. Picture yourself as an actor stepping into someone else's shoes—not just wearing them but really feeling the ground beneath them. Designing empathy role-play scenarios can be a fun and enlightening experience. Imagine you're in a workplace setting, playing the role of a colleague who's overwhelmed with tasks. As you navigate this scenario, you'll gain insights into their emotional landscape, experiencing firsthand the pressures they face. Once the role-play ends, take a moment to reflect on what you've learned. What emotions surfaced? How did the experience change your perspective? This reflection is where the magic happens, turning a simple exercise into a profound lesson in empathy.

Now, let's talk about empathic listening circles. Think of a bunch of friends sitting in a relaxing room, each taking turns to share their stories while the others truly listen—without judgment. These circles are about creating a safe space where everyone feels heard and valued. Structuring a listening circle session involves setting clear guidelines, such as no interruptions and maintaining confidentiality. The heart of these sessions lies in offering constructive feedback. Instead of saying, "I think you should have done this," try, "I felt you were really brave sharing that." This approach affirms the speaker's experience and fosters a sense of trust and connection within the group.

Storytelling, too, is a fantastic way to cultivate empathy. Think of it as opening a window into someone else's world. When you share your stories, you invite others to walk alongside you, experiencing triumphs and challenges. Use storytelling prompts to guide these narratives, focusing on moments that have shaped or taught you something significant. As you listen to others' stories, consider your emotional responses. Did a particular story make you smile, or did it bring a tear to your eye? Analyzing these reactions helps you understand your own empathetic tendencies and where there's room for growth.

Finally, there's empathy journaling. It's like keeping a diary of your empathic encounters. Each entry can serve as a snapshot of your inter-actions, capturing moments where you felt connected and those where you struggled. Use journaling prompts like "Describe a time when you felt deeply understood" or "Reflect on a conversation that challenged your empathy." Over time, you'll notice patterns and themes, tracking your progress and uncovering insights about your empathic journey. This practice enhances your understanding of empathy and encour-ages continuous self-reflection and development.

Reflection Exercise: Empathy Journaling Prompts

- Describe a recent interaction where you felt empathy. What emotions did you experience?
- Reflect on a situation where empathy was challenging. What made it difficult?
- Identify a moment when someone showed you empathy. How did it impact you?

These exercises are about building empathy and transforming how you relate to others. As you practice, you'll become more attuned to the emotions and experiences of those around you, fostering deeper and more meaningful connections.

4.2 THE FEEDBACK LOOP: PRACTICING CONSTRUCTIVE DIALOGUE

Imagine a conversation where both parties leave feeling heard, understood, and respected. That's the beauty of a feedback loop. It's not just about tossing words back and forth like a game of verbal ping-pong. A feedback loop is a dynamic exchange that strengthens communication and understanding. At its core, it involves giving and receiving feedback in a way that promotes growth and clarity. Effective feedback is specific, timely, and focused on behavior rather than personality. It's the difference between saying, "You always interrupt," and "I noticed you cut me off twice this morning." The latter opens a door for understanding and improvement. The benefits of a feedback loop are immense. It creates a space where ideas can flourish, misunderstandings are minimized, and relationships are strengthened. It's like having a conversation with mirrors, reflecting back not just what is said but what is understood.

So, how do you give feedback without sounding like a nagging parent or a dissatisfied customer? One technique is the "sh!t sandwich" approach. Start with a positive observation, then address the area for improvement, and finish with encouragement. It softens the blow and ensures your message doesn't feel like an attack. Practice this by role-playing with a friend or colleague, focusing on delivering feedback that is both constructive and supportive. Equally important is learning to receive feedback gracefully. It's tempting to get defensive, but instead, take a deep breath and listen with the intent to understand, not to reply. Ask questions for clarity and thank the person for their insights. It's like eating your vegetables—not always fun, but good for you.

Feedback loops aren't just for the office; they're like universal keys that unlock better communication in every setting. At work, they can transform team dynamics. Consider a company that implemented regular feedback sessions, not just from managers but from peers. This open dialogue increased trust and innovation, as employees felt their voices were truly valued. In personal relationships, feedback loops act as a pressure release valve, allowing partners to express concerns before they build up into full-blown arguments. Tailoring your feedback approach to different audiences is crucial. You might need a gentler touch with family, while colleagues might appreciate directness. It's about knowing your audience and adjusting your delivery accordingly.

Creating situations where feedback is welcomed and valued involves more than just saying, "Tell me what you think." It means building a foundation of trust. This requires keeping an open door for discussions and showing that you value and act on the feedback you receive. Establishing norms and guidelines for feedback can help set the tone. For instance, agree that all feedback will be given with the intent to support, not criticize. Regularly scheduled feedback sessions can normalize the practice, making it a routine part of your interactions rather than a dreaded event.

Take a moment to reflect on a recent conversation in which you received feedback. Consider how you responded and what you could do differently next time. Jot down any insights about the feedback itself and how it was delivered. This reflection can guide you in giving and receiving feedback more effectively in the future.

When feedback becomes a natural part of your communication toolkit, it transforms interactions from mere exchanges to opportunities for connection and growth. It's about creating a dialogue that's not just constructive but also transformative, paving the way for better relationships and deeper understanding.

4.3 LISTENING JOURNALS: TRACKING PROGRESS AND INSIGHTS

Have you ever had one of those days where you think, "Wow, I was really on point in that conversation!"? And then there are days when you wonder if you even heard half of what was said. That's where a listening journal comes into play. It's like a diary but for your ears. Keeping a listening journal isn't just about jotting down random thoughts; it's a tool for growth. By documenting your listening experiences, you gain insights into your strengths and areas needing a little TLC. Think of it as a personal cheat sheet for becoming the listener you've always wanted to be. The objective is simple: track your progress, spot patterns, and determine what works best. Some folks go for a digital journal, while others love the tactile feel of pen and paper. Whatever your style, the goal is to have a dedicated space to reflect on your listening journey.

Starting a listening journal is easier than you think. Begin by deciding what you'll document. Maybe you want to capture those "aha!" moments when you realized something new or jot down instances where you struggled to stay focused. Consider prompts like "What did I learn from today's conversations?" or "How did I handle distractions?" These prompts help you dig deeper rather than just scratching the surface. As for how often you should write, that's entirely up to you. Some people prefer a daily habit, while others find weekly entries work fine. Set a schedule that feels realistic and stick to it. The consistency will pay off; trust me.

Once you've got some entries, it's time to play detective. Flip through your journal and look for patterns. Are there specific situations where you excel at listening? Maybe you're more engaged during one-on-one chats but zone out in big meetings. Recognizing these patterns helps you identify your listening sweet spots and the areas that need more work. Look for recurring themes, like topics that capture your interest or distractions that pull you away. Reflect on these observations and consider what they reveal about your listening habits. Are you a good listener when you're relaxed but not so much when stressed? Gaining this insight is like having a personal roadmap to guide your listening improvement.

With all this valuable information at your fingertips, you can now set specific listening goals. Use your journal insights to create actionable objectives. For example, if you notice you struggle with staying focused during virtual meetings, set a goal to minimize distractions by closing unnecessary tabs or muting notifications. Goal-setting exercises can be as simple as writing down what you want to achieve and breaking it into smaller, manageable steps. Tracking your progress regularly means reviewing the entries in your journal and adjusting your goals as needed. This process creates a feedback loop where your journal not only documents your journey but also guides your future growth.

A listening journal is your personal listening lab, a place to experiment, reflect, and grow. It's about creating a habit of self-awareness and continuous improvement. So grab your journal and start listening with intention.

4.4 INTERACTIVE SCENARIOS: APPLYING SKILLS IN REAL LIFE

Imagine you're at a dinner party, and the conversation shifts to a topic you're not familiar with. Suddenly, you're nodding along, trying to piece together the discussion without giving away your cluelessness. We've all been there, and scenarios like these make practicing listening skills in real-life settings so valuable. Designing realistic scenarios for practice is like setting up a playground for your listening muscles. The key is to create situations that mimic everyday challenges. Imagine you're trying to follow a fast-paced meeting, juggling multiple voices and opinions. This requires you to focus on key points while filtering out the noise. Effective scenario design involves crafting situations that are relatable, challenging, and varied enough to push your skills to new heights.

Once your scenario is set up, it's time to dive in. Engaging with these scenarios requires more than just going through the motions. It's about actively participating, staying present, and reflecting on your performance. Techniques for these scenario-based learning can include role reversals, where you switch roles with someone else to see things from their perspective. This not only hones your listening skills but also boosts empathy. After running through a scenario, take a moment to reflect. Ask yourself questions like: What did I do well? Where did I struggle? What can I improve next time? This reflection helps solidify your learning and guides your ongoing development.

Group activities can take your learning to the next level. Encourage a few friends or colleagues to join you in scenario exercises. Picture a group exercise where everyone plays different roles in a customer service situation. This makes the practice more dynamic and allows you to learn from each other's experiences. Structuring these group activities involves setting clear objectives and guidelines, ensuring everyone knows their role and the goals of the session. After the exercise, hold a debriefing session. It's like a post-game analysis where everyone shares insights and feedback. This collaborative learning environment fosters growth and strengthens communication within the group.

Evaluating your performance in scenarios is crucial for tracking progress. Set criteria for assessing listening effectiveness, such as recalling key points, interpreting nonverbal cues, and responding appropriately. Feedback mechanisms can include peer reviews, where participants provide constructive feedback on each other's performance. This feedback loop not only highlights areas for improvement but also builds a supportive learning community. Regularly assessing your performance lets you understand your strengths and areas needing attention, allowing you to tailor your practice for maximum impact.

Interactive scenarios give you a unique and engaging method to apply listening skills in real-life contexts. They create a safe space to experiment, learn, and grow, transforming theoretical knowledge into practical application. By incorporating scenarios into your practice, you'll improve your listening skills and build confidence and resilience in handling diverse communication challenges. So gather a few friends, set up a scenario, and see how much you can learn and grow together.

SAY SOMETHING THAT ACTUALLY HELPS

How to Make a Bigger Impact Than Just Reading

"Being heard is cool. Helping others feel heard? That's next-level." — Some guy smarter than me

Let's be real—people who do things just to help others are the ones who actually make the world less annoying. So, here's your shot to do something small that makes a big difference.

You found this book for a reason. Maybe you're working on your relationships, trying to stop steamrolling conversations, or just want people to stop calling you "that guy." Whatever the reason, you've started the work—and that's awesome.

Now, want to help someone else do the same?

Most people pick a book based on the reviews. Not the cover. Not the title. The reviews. So yeah, **your review matters** more than you think.

Think of who your review might help:

- Someone who keeps interrupting but actually wants to change
- Someone who never learned how to listen, but now wants to get better at it
- Someone who's sick of surface-level convos and wants to actually connect
- Someone who might not hear this message unless YOU tell them it was worth it

And it only takes like a minute. Less than the time it takes to scroll past three dumb TikToks.

READY TO PAY IT FORWARD?

Scan this link and drop a review:

[https://www.amazon.com/review/review-your-purchases/?asin=BOOKASIN]

(Or just copy/paste it like it's 2003—whatever works.)

Or Scan this QR code:

If you made it this far, you're my kind of person. Thank you for reading, for listening, and for helping someone else start their own journey.

– JD Vaughn

CHAPTER 5
ADVANCED TECHNIQUES FOR DIALOGUE BALANCE

HAVE you ever been in a conversation where one person dominates the entire discussion, leaving everyone else politely nodding while their inner thoughts are screaming, "Can I please say something, too?" It's like being stuck in a never-ending monologue, hoping for a commercial break so you can finally chime in. Enter the Two-Minute Rule—a simple yet effective tool to level the playing field and ensure everyone gets their moment in the spotlight. Think of it as the egg timer of conversation, giving each person a fair chance to speak without turning the discussion into an endless loop of chatter.

The Two-Minute Rule is a nifty little concept designed to balance speaking time during conversations in casual chats and formal meetings. The idea is straightforward: each speaker gets only two minutes to share their thoughts before someone else's turn. This creates a rhythm that keeps the conversation fresh and engaging, ensuring no one hogs the mic too long. It's a musical duet where each person sings their part, creating a harmonious exchange that encourages active listening and vibrant dialogue. By doing so, everyone's voice gets heard, and the flow of ideas becomes more dynamic and inclusive.

Implementing the Two-Minute Rule in conversations is more manageable. First, set a friendly reminder or use your phone on vibrate as a timer to keep track of the two-minute intervals. This isn't about strict enforcement but rather a gentle nudge to keep things moving. When speaking, aim to convey your main points succinctly, focusing on clarity rather than cramming in every detail. For smooth transitions, you can pass the metaphorical baton by summarizing your thoughts and inviting the next person to share theirs. It's like a game of conversational tag, where everyone gets a turn to speak without fear of being interrupted or overshadowed.

Adapting the Two-Minute Rule to various contexts requires finesse. In informal settings, like a friendly chat over coffee, the rule can be relaxed, allowing for a more organic flow. Here, it's more about being mindful of not monopolizing the conversation rather than rigidly timing each contribution. In contrast, formal meetings can benefit from a more structured approach. Setting clear guidelines and gently reminding participants of the rules can help maintain focus and prevent the discussion from veering off course. It's like setting the stage for a well-rehearsed play, where everyone knows their lines and cues, resulting in a seamless performance.

While the Two-Minute Rule offers many benefits, it's not without its challenges. The best part? Everyone can speak without being steamrolled by the loudest person in the room. This fosters a sense of inclusion and collaboration, making the conversation more enriching and diverse. However, resistance to structured speaking times can arise, especially from those who prefer a more free-flowing dialogue. To address this, it's important to emphasize the rule's purpose—creating a balanced conversation that values every voice. Encourage open discussions about the rule's implementation, inviting feedback and suggestions to refine the approach. This collaborative effort can transform initial skepticism into enthusiastic participation, paving the way for more meaningful and productive exchanges.

Test out the Two-Minute Rule with a friend or colleague. Set a two-minute timer and take turns sharing your thoughts on a chosen topic. Notice how this structure influences the conversation dynamics. Reflect on how it feels to have dedicated time to speak and listen. Consider incorporating this practice into your future discussions to enhance dialogue balance.

Navigating the complexities of conversation requires skill and intention. By incorporating the Two-Minute Rule, we can create a more balanced and inclusive space for dialogue where every voice is heard and valued.

5.1 OPEN-ENDED QUESTIONS: ENCOURAGING DEEPER DIALOGUE

Imagine you're at a backyard barbecue, chatting with a neighbor. You ask, "Did you like the movie?" and they reply with a simple "Yes." End of conversation, right? Now, picture asking instead, "What did you think of the movie?" Suddenly, you're going through their thoughts, opinions, and experiences. This is the magic of open-ended questions. They invite elaboration, turning a mundane exchange into a rich dialogue. Open-ended questions are like keys that unlock the treasure chest of thoughts, revealing layers of insight that yes/no questions simply can't reach. They steer conversations away from dead ends, inviting exploration and discovery.

Crafting effective open-ended questions is an art worth mastering. It starts with being curious. Imagine you're a detective; your job is to uncover the stories behind the words. Change the questions that can be answered with a simple yes or no to questions that require more thought. Instead of asking, "Did you enjoy your trip?" try, "What was the most memorable part of your trip?" This subtle shift in phrasing encourages the other person to share more, transforming the conversation into a journey through their experiences. When forming these questions, use words like "how," "what," "why," and "tell me about." These words naturally lead to more detailed responses, opening the door to meaningful dialogue.

Adding open-ended questions to your conversations can make them more engaging and meaningful. Begin by actively listening to the other person's cues. If they mention a recent project at work, instead of nodding along, ask, "What was the most challenging part of that project?" This shows actual interest and encourages them to share more. Another technique is to use open-ended questions as a bridge between topics. If a friend talks about a new hobby, ask, "What inspired you to start that?" This not only keeps the conversation flowing but also deepens the connection between you. It's like adding layers to a cake, each question revealing another layer of the person's thoughts and feelings.

The impact of open-ended questions on dialogue is profound, but how do you know if you're asking the right ones? Evaluating their effectiveness involves paying attention to the depth and engagement of the conversation. After asking a question, observe the other person's response. Are they animated and thoughtful, or do they seem unsure and hesitant? Feedback like this offers a clearer picture of how your questions are received and whether they prompt real engagement. Reflect on the outcomes—did the conversation delve into new territories, or did it stay on the surface? Adjust your approach based on this reflection, fine-tuning your questions to encourage even deeper exploration. It's like being a conversational gardener, pruning and nurturing your questions to foster growth and connection.

To make open-ended questions a natural part of your dialogue toolkit, consider incorporating them into your daily interactions. Challenge yourself to replace one closed question with an open-ended one each day. Observe the difference it makes in your conversations. Keep a mental checklist of your favorite questions and use them to spark deeper discussions with friends, family, and colleagues. As you become more comfortable, you'll find that these questions not only enrich your dialogues but also strengthen your relationships, creating a tapestry of connections woven from shared stories and insights.

5.2 ECHOING AND PARAPHRASING: TECHNIQUES FOR CLARIFICATION

Have you ever been in a conversation where you nod along only to realize you missed the point? It's a common pitfall that echoing and paraphrasing can help avoid. These techniques are like having a built-in GPS for conversations, ensuring you stay on the right path. So, what exactly are echoing and paraphrasing? Simply put, echoing involves repeating a speaker's words back to them, perhaps for emphasis or to show attentiveness. Paraphrasing, on the other hand, is about expressing the speaker's message in your own words, confirming you grasp their meaning. While echoing mirrors words, paraphrasing captures the essence of the message. Both techniques act as check-points, verifying understanding and preventing miscommunication.

How can you effectively paraphrase without sounding like a record-ing? First, listen actively to absorb the speaker's message. Then, rephrase what they've said, focusing on the main points. For example, if a colleague explains a complicated process, respond with, "So, you're saying we need to complete step one before moving on to step two, right?" This confirms your understanding and allows the speaker to correct any potential errors. It's also a great way to show you're engaged and truly interested in what they say. By practicing this regu-larly, you'll become more adept at capturing the speaker's intent, making your conversations more meaningful and productive.

Echoing, while seemingly simple, is a powerful tool for validation and clarification. Imagine your friend sharing a challenging day at work, saying, "I was just so overwhelmed with the deadlines." You could echo with, "Overwhelmed with deadlines, huh?" This not only shows you're listening but invites them to elaborate if they choose. Echoing can also be used to highlight key points or emotions, offering the speaker the chance to expand on their thoughts. It's like holding up a mirror, reflecting back the speaker's words and feelings, allowing them to see their message more clearly. Through this process, you facilitate a deeper connection and open the door for further dialogue.

Echoing and paraphrasing are powerful tools that can improve communication on multiple levels. They help confirm that both people understand each other, which goes a long way in avoiding confusion and preventing unnecessary conflict. When you actually use this stuff, people notice—and they're way more likely to trust you and open up. When someone feels truly heard, they're more likely to trust and open up, leading to richer and more authentic conversations. It's like adding glue to the relationship, strengthening the bond through shared under-standing. By mastering these skills, you'll find that your interactions become more engaging, insightful, and fulfilling.

Practice Exercise: Paraphrasing Scenarios

Think of a recent conversation where you felt unsure about the message. Replay it in your mind, and try paraphrasing the main points using your own words. Consider how the speaker might respond to your paraphrase. Write it down and reflect on how this exercise clarifies the speaker's intent. Practice this with different scenarios to enhance your paraphrasing skills.

Understanding and applying echoing and paraphrasing might seem straightforward, but their impact is profound. They transform ordinary conversations into meaningful exchanges rooted in clarity and mutual respect. As you incorporate these techniques into your communication toolkit, you'll notice a remarkable difference in the quality of your interactions.

5.3 MANAGING DOMINANCE AND RETICENCE IN GROUP SETTINGS

Ever sat in a meeting where one person talks so much you start wondering if they've got a personal vendetta against silence? Or maybe you've seen someone so quiet that you question if they're practicing to audition as a mime. These are the dynamics of dominance and reticence in group settings. Dominance often appears as someone who jumps in at every opportunity, steering the conversation and leaving little room for others. They might interrupt or go on long monologues, their enthusiasm sometimes overshadowing quieter voices. On the flip side, you have the reticent participants. These folks might sit back, nodding along, contributing only when directly asked. They might be shy, unsure, or simply overwhelmed by the louder voices in the room. Both dynamics can skew dialogue balance, making it tricky to hear all perspectives.

Balancing participation in group discussions is like hosting a potluck where everyone needs to bring a dish. You don't want just one person bringing all the food while another brings nothing. Start by moderating dominant voices. Set ground rules that encourage turn-taking, reminding everyone that the best conversations are a shared space. You might say, "Let's hear from someone who hasn't spoken yet." This creates room for the quieter members to step in. For those reticent souls, create opportunities for them to shine. Encourage them beforehand or gently nudge them during the conversation. "I'd love to hear your thoughts on this" can be a simple invitation that opens the door. It's about creating a balance that ensures everyone's dish—er, voice—gets a place at the table.

Making a space inclusive isn't just about keeping things even—it's about making sure everyone knows they matter and their voice counts. Techniques for inclusive facilitation involve setting a welcoming tone from the get-go. Start by establishing group norms that emphasize respect and equal participation. This could be as simple as agreeing that no idea is too small or silly to share. Encourage active listening by asking participants to acknowledge others' contributions before adding their own. This approach not only validates each speaker but also enriches the dialogue with diverse perspectives. A facilitator guides the conversation gently, ensuring it doesn't veer too far off course while still allowing for organic flow.

Assessing group interaction dynamics over time is crucial to refining how discussions unfold. Facilitating a group means paying attention to how the conversation is unfolding and making adjustments when needed to keep it healthy and inclusive. Use group dynamics assessment tools to gauge participation levels and identify any patterns hindering effective communication. This could involve simple surveys where participants can anonymously share their thoughts on the discussion process. Are there voices that consistently dominate? Are some members always quiet? Gathering this feedback provides valuable insights into how the group functions. It allows facilitators to adapt their strategies, ensuring the environment remains conducive to collaborative and meaningful dialogue.

The beauty of managing dominance and reticence lies in transforming what could be a cacophony of voices into a harmonious exchange. By recognizing the signs of both dynamics and employing strategies to balance them, we create spaces where everyone feels empowered to speak up. It's about fostering an environment where every participant, whether naturally dominant or reticent, can contribute to the conversation. Through inclusive facilitation, setting norms, and regular assessment, we cultivate a dialogue that is not only balanced but also enriching, paving the way for more effective and fulfilling group interactions.

5.4 THE ART OF SILENCE IN COMMUNICATION

Silence. It's that moment in a conversation that can feel like an eternity. The clock seems to slow down, and you might wonder if everyone else hears the same deafening quiet. Yet, when used with intention, silence becomes a powerful tool in communication. It can emphasize points, allowing the weight of what's been said to settle in truly. Think of it like those dramatic pauses in movies that make the next scene all the more impactful. It's not about awkwardness; it's about giving space for reflection and allowing ideas to breathe. Silence isn't just the absence of sound—it's a canvas upon which thoughts can be painted, offering clarity in a conversation that is sometimes cluttered with too much noise.

Incorporating silence into your dialogue might feel counterintuitive at first. After all, aren't conversations supposed to be filled with words? But consider this: Silence gives you a moment to gather your thoughts, ensuring that your next words are thoughtful rather than rushed. A well-timed pause can prevent misunderstandings, allowing others to process what has been said. It can also give the other person a gentle nudge to contribute more, inviting them to fill the space. Timing is key here. Having a brief pause after you've asked a question can encourage deeper responses, while a longer silence during a heated moment can diffuse tension. It's like seasoning—enough can enhance the flavor, but too much can overwhelm it.

Practicing silence involves more than just biting your tongue. It requires a level of comfort with quiet that many of us aren't used to. Start with small exercises. If you pause for a few seconds before responding in conversations, it is one method to try. Notice how this changes the flow and depth of the discussion. It might feel awkward initially, like trying to dance without music, but with practice, it becomes a natural and effective part of your communication repertoire.

Reflecting on these moments of silence can also be enlightening. Ask yourself how the pause affected the interaction and what insights emerged during that quiet space. It's like watching a painting come to life as the colors are added individually.

For many, silence is something to be avoided, a void to be filled. However, overcoming the discomfort of silence can transform how you engage with others. It's about shifting your mindset from fearing silence to seeing it as a strategic pause. This shift allows you to use silence to enhance understanding and build constructive rapport. Reflective exercises help ease this transition. Try sitting with your thoughts for a few minutes each day—no pressure or judgment. It makes those quiet moments in real conversations feel way less awkward.

Evaluating silence's impact is like assessing a film's background music. You might not notice it consciously, but it sets the tone and influences the experience. Reflect on how silence has shaped your recent interactions. Did it lead to deeper insights or create space for more meaningful dialogue? Grab a notebook and track what silence actually does in your conversations—does it help, hurt, or just make things weird? Over time, you'll develop a keen sense of when and how to use silence to its fullest effect, turning an awkward pause into a powerful tool for connection.

As we wrap up our exploration of dialogue balance, remember that silence is just one of many tools you can use. It's the quiet partner in a conversation, allowing space for reflection and connection. In the next chapter, we'll explore empathy and understanding, exploring how these elements can further enrich your communication and deepen your relationships.

CHAPTER 6
DEVELOPING EMPATHY AND UNDERSTANDING

IMAGINE YOU'RE AT A PARTY, and someone tells you about their pet iguana, who, in their opinion, is the most misunderstood creature ever. Your first thought might be, "Iguanas? Really?" But what if, instead of dismissing it, you tried to see the world through their eyes— or even through the eyes of that iguana? Welcome to the wild world of empathy, where walking in someone else's shoes might mean getting to know a pet lizard's daily struggles. Empathy is a game-changer in how we connect with others. It's about understanding different perspectives, not just nodding along. When you embrace this, you unlock a deeper level of communication that can transform relationships.

Let's talk about perspective-taking. This is where you deliberately try to see things from another person's point of view—like putting on their glasses to see what they see. Imagine a scenario where you're in a heated debate about pineapple on pizza. Instead of digging your heels in (because, let's face it, pineapple is controversial), try stepping into the other person's mindset. Why might they adore this fruit-topped delight? It's not just about the taste; maybe it reminds them of family pizza nights. This shift can break down barriers and foster genuine understanding. Empathy mapping is a useful technique here. Picture a map that charts out someone's feelings, needs, and challenges, helping you clearly navigate their world.

Now, let's get into some empathy exercises. One exercise involves imagining alternate life experiences. Picture yourself as a barista dealing with the morning rush. Customers aren't just buying coffee; they're battling morning grumpiness, and you're their hero. Reflecting on these scenarios can reveal your own biases. Maybe you've never considered how life looks from behind the counter. This exercise reminds us that everyone has their own battles, and seeing those can change how we interact with them.

Empathy Journaling Prompt

- Reflect on a recent interaction where you struggled to understand the other person's perspective. What assumptions did you make? How might their experiences differ from your own?

Empathy isn't just about getting someone else's story—it's about learning more about yourself. When you really try to see life from someone else's shoes, the walls blocking empathy start to crumble. You become more aware of emotional nuances and how they shape interactions. This awareness is like a light bulb moment, illuminating areas where you can grow and connect more deeply with others.

Evaluating your progress in developing empathy is crucial. Reflect on your experiences and consider keeping an empathy journal. This can be a space to document moments of connection and those where empathy felt elusive. Ask yourself, "What did I learn about myself? How would I feel in their shoes?" Feedback from others can also be enlightening. Invite your friends or colleagues to share their perspectives on your empathic skills. This feedback loop helps you see how your efforts are perceived and where to improve.

Empathy isn't a fixed trait; it's a skill you can cultivate and refine. Deliberately practicing empathy opens you to deeper connections and enriched relationships.

6.1 EMOTIONAL RESONANCE: CONNECTING BEYOND WORDS

Have you ever been in a conversation where words seemed to fade into the background, and you *knew* what the other person felt? That's emotional resonance at play. It's like tuning into a friend's frequency, catching the subtle signals that words alone can't convey. Emotional resonance allows us to connect on a level that goes beyond verbal communication. When a friend shares a tough day or the shared laughter, the nod of understanding lights up a room. These moments create a sense of closeness, making interactions more meaningful and genuine. Emotional resonance is about attuning to others' feelings and acknowledging them even when they're not explicitly stated.

To enhance emotional resonance, you can practice being actively present. This means being fully engaged in the moment, not just physically but emotionally. Think of it as tuning in to a radio station, where you adjust the dial until the music comes in clear. One way to do this is through attunement exercises with partners. Spend a few minutes each day focusing solely on your partner's emotions. Listen to their words, but also observe their body language, tone, and expressions. Try to feel what they feel, whether it's joy, frustration, or excitement. Active presence practices, such as maintaining eye contact and minimizing distractions, also help you engage more deeply, ensuring you're not just hearing but truly understanding.

When you actually connect with someone on an emotional level, it changes everything. Trust gets stronger, conversations flow better, and people feel safe enough to be real with you. It's that unspoken vibe that keeps people grounded when things get messy and boosts the energy when things are going right. In work settings, emotional resonance changes the game. When people feel seen and heard, collaboration isn't forced—it just happens. Teams click, communication flows, and ideas actually get traction. It creates a space where people aren't afraid to speak up, throw out bold ideas, or admit when something's off—and that's where real progress starts.

However, achieving emotional resonance isn't always a walk in the park. Barriers can arise, creating emotional disconnects that can strain relationships. These disconnects often stem from stress, misunderstanding, or simply not taking the time to fully engage. To overcome these barriers, focus on building emotional awareness. Your own emotions need to be recognized and understood for their impact on your interactions. It's like having a GPS for your feelings, guiding you through emotional terrain. Addressing emotional disconnects requires patience and empathy. Take the time to acknowledge any tensions and address them openly. This might mean asking questions to clarify feelings or taking a break to cool off before continuing a discussion.

Building emotional awareness is a lifelong practice. It involves tuning into your emotional responses and reflecting on how they influence your interactions. Keeping a journal to document your emotional experiences is something to consider. Reflect on moments when you felt emotionally connected and those when you didn't. What factors contributed to these outcomes? How can you improve your emotional awareness moving forward? This ongoing reflection helps you recognize patterns and make adjustments, enhancing your ability to resonate with others emotionally.

6.2 BUILDING RAPPORT THROUGH REFLECTIVE LISTENING

Ever found yourself nodding along in a conversation, only to realize you missed half of what was said? It happens. This is where reflective listening swoops in like a superhero saving the day. Reflective listening is all about validating others' experiences and building understanding. It's the secret sauce that helps you forge a solid rapport with just about anyone. When you practice reflective listening, you're not just a passive ear but an active participant, echoing back what you've heard to show you truly get it. Think of it as holding up a mirror, reflecting the speaker's emotions and words so they know you're tuned in. Imagine your friend venting about a tough day. Instead of mumbling a distracted "uh-huh," you might say, "Sounds like you had a challenging time." This simple act of acknowledgment shows empathy and helps build trust.

To practice reflective listening effectively, start with mirroring emotions. This doesn't mean mimicking someone's feelings like a parrot. Instead, it's about conveying understanding through your tone and body language. If a colleague shares their frustration over a project, mirror that emotion by acknowledging their stress with a sympathetic nod or a gentle, understanding tone. Summarizing key points is another powerful technique. After listening to someone's story, try summarizing the main ideas back to them. It might sound like this: "So, if I understand correctly, you're feeling overwhelmed by the tight deadline?" This not only confirms you're on the same page but also gives the speaker a chance to clarify any misunderstandings.

It can be a fun and effective way using role-play scenarios to hone your reflective listening skills. Gather a group of friends or colleagues and take turns playing different roles. One person shares a story while others practice reflective listening techniques. It might feel like adult improv, but it's a great way to get hands-on experience. You can even spice things up by throwing in unexpected twists, like having the speaker switch topics mid-sentence. This keeps everyone on their toes and sharpens their listening abilities. Group exercises in rapport building are also valuable. Try setting up a listening circle where each person shares a brief story. The rest of the group jumps in by practicing reflective listening—repeating back the main points and matching the speaker's tone and emotions to show they're actually tuned in. This collaborative approach not only strengthens individual skills but also fosters a sense of camaraderie and support.

Assessing your progress in building rapport through reflective listening is crucial. One way to do this is by seeking feedback from your conversation partners. After a chat, ask them how they felt about your listening. Were they comfortable? Did they feel understood? This feedback can be eye-opening, revealing areas where you excel and where there's room for improvement. Self-assessment is another valuable tool. Reflect on your recent interactions and consider questions like, "Did I successfully mirror their emotions?" or "Did I accurately summarize their main points?" Keep a journal to track your progress and identify patterns in your listening habits. This self-awareness helps you fine-tune your skills and ensures you're continually growing.

Reflective listening is more than just a technique; it's a way to connect with others on a deeper level, validating their experiences and building trust. By honing these skills, you become a better listener and enrich your relationships, making your interactions more meaningful and rewarding.

6.3 TRUST AND VULNERABILITY IN CONVERSATIONS

Imagine you're on a first date, and both of you are playing it safe, sticking to polite chitchat about the weather or that new restaurant everyone's raving about. Now, picture a different scenario: you share a personal anecdote about the time you accidentally walked into a glass door, and it's met with an equally embarrassing story from the other side of the table. Suddenly, the air feels lighter, the laughter is genuine, and you're more relaxed. What just happened was a moment of trust and vulnerability—two cornerstones of meaningful conversation. Trust is necessary for us to be open, knowing our words won't be used against us. Vulnerability, however, is showing up as our true selves, even when it feels risky. Together, they create a fertile ground for honest dialogue and deeper connections.

Trust doesn't just show up—it's earned, little by little. You build it by doing the small things right: keeping your word, showing up, and not running your mouth when someone shares something personal. It takes time, but if you're consistent, people start to feel like they can actually count on you. That's when the real connection starts to grow. These actions might seem minor, but they lay the groundwork for more significant exchanges. Consider the simple act of listening without interrupting. By giving someone the space to speak, you show them they matter, fostering trust bit by bit. Trust also grows when you acknowledge your mistakes. Admitting when you're wrong is a powerful way to demonstrate authenticity and reliability, strengthening the trust between you and the other person.

But trust alone isn't enough. Vulnerability is the magic ingredient that amplifies connection. Sharing personal experiences and expressing emotions can be intimidating but incredibly rewarding. It's like peeling back layers of an onion, revealing more of who you are—tears and all.

To foster vulnerability, start by sharing stories that hold meaning for you. It doesn't have to be a grand revelation; it could be a childhood memory or a recent challenge. These narratives create a bridge between you and the listener, inviting them to share their own stories. Exercises in emotional expression can help here. Practice expressing your feelings in a journal or with a trusted friend. This practice builds confidence and makes vulnerability feel less daunting in conversations.

However, diving headfirst into vulnerability without boundaries can lead to uncomfortable waters. It's crucial to balance vulnerability with healthy boundaries. Setting boundaries means knowing your limits and respecting the limits of others. It's like having a fence around your garden—not to keep people out, but to protect what's within. In conversations, establish boundaries by being clear about what you're comfortable sharing. If a topic feels too personal, it's okay to steer the conversation elsewhere. Recognize and respect the other person's boundaries, too. Pay attention to cues like body language or changes in tone that signal discomfort, and adjust your approach accordingly.

Assessing the dynamics of trust and vulnerability in your relationships is an ongoing process. Reflect on past interactions and consider how trust and vulnerability played a role. Were there times when you held back out of fear? Or moments when you felt safe enough to be your authentic self? This reflection helps you understand the balance between trust and vulnerability in your conversations. Seeking feedback from those you trust can also provide valuable insights. Ask them how they perceive your openness and whether they feel comfortable sharing with you. This feedback offers a fresh perspective and highlights areas for growth. Trust and vulnerability are like dance partners, moving together to create a rhythm that enriches communication and connection.

6.4 NAVIGATING DIFFICULT EMOTIONS WITH COMPASSION

Picture this: you're in the middle of a heated conversation, and suddenly, emotions flare up like a wildfire. Before you know it, words are flying, and you're caught in the storm, wondering how you got there. Difficult emotions, like anger or frustration, can hijack conversations and lead to misunderstandings. They're those uninvited guests that crash the party and make everything awkward. But here's the thing: addressing these emotions with compassion can transform the entire interaction. When you approach challenging emotions with empathy, you create a space where feelings are acknowledged and understood, not dismissed or ignored.

When faced with a surge of emotions from someone else, it's tempting to react defensively. Instead, try responding with empathetic listening. This involves tuning in to the emotions behind the words, not just the words themselves. Imagine your friend is venting about their terrible day. Rather than jumping in with advice or trying to fix things, simply listen. Nod, maintain eye contact, and offer affirming responses like "I can see why you'd feel that way." These cues show you're present and genuinely care about their feelings. Offering compassionate support goes hand-in-hand with empathetic listening. Sometimes, people just need to know they're not alone. You might say, "That sounds really tough. I'm here for you." It's a small gesture, but it can mean the world to someone who's feeling overwhelmed.

Of course, managing your own emotions during these interactions is equally important. It's like being on an airplane when they tell you to put on your mask before helping others. You can't be there for someone else if you're spiraling yourself. Start by practicing breathing exercises for emotional regulation. When you feel your emotions bubbling up, take a long, deep breath, hold it for a few moments, and then slowly exhale. This easy exercise can calm your nervous system and help you maintain composure. Reflecting on emotional triggers is another helpful practice. After a challenging conversation, take a moment to think about what set you off. Was it a specific word, tone, or topic? Understanding your triggers helps you prepare for future interactions and approach them with greater awareness.

Improving your compassionate communication skills isn't a one-and-done deal. It's an ongoing process that involves both feedback and self-reflection. After a conversation, consider asking the other person how they felt about your response. Did they feel heard and supported? This feedback can be invaluable, offering insights into areas where you can grow. Self-reflection is equally important. Spend some time thinking about how you handled the conversation. Were there moments when you could have been more empathetic? What did you do well? Maintaining a journal will help to keep track of your progress and identify response patterns.

Navigating difficult emotions with compassion is like learning to dance in the rain. It might be challenging at first, but with practice, you can move through the storm with grace and understanding. Addressing emotions with empathy improves communication and deepens connections with others. As we close this chapter, remember that these skills are valuable tools for becoming a more compassionate listener. The next chapter will explore how these listening skills apply in the ever-evolving digital landscape, where communication takes on new forms and challenges.

CHAPTER 7
DIGITAL LISTENING AND VIRTUAL COMMUNICATION

PICTURE THIS: you're in a virtual meeting, staring at a screen full of Brady Bunch-style squares, each one containing a colleague who might or might not be paying attention. Welcome to the brave new world of digital communication, where your laptop is your boardroom, and your cat is your most frequent co-worker. As more of our interactions shift from face-to-face to screen-to-screen, understanding how to connect in this digital realm genuinely is more important than ever. The stakes are high; after all, no one wants to be the person who accidentally unmutes themselves while singing along to their Spotify playlist during a serious business meeting.

Despite the challenges, video calls have become essential in personal and professional settings. Unlike face-to-face conversations that offer clear body language and vocal cues, video calls require you to pay attention to a different set of signals. Visual and auditory signals are crucial in these interactions, offering subtle clues about engagement and understanding. For example, a head nod or a smile can indicate agreement, while a furrowed brow might signal confusion or disagreement. Similarly, auditory cues, such as a thoughtful "hmm" or an enthusiastic "yes," can convey interest or comprehension. However, these cues often get muddled through the pixelated world of video calls, making it vital to adapt our communication strategies.

So, how do you make sure you're sending and receiving these cues effectively? First, let's talk about eye contact—or at least the video call version. Instead of staring at your colleague's image on the screen, try looking directly at the camera. It might feel odd, like you're trying to win a staring contest with your webcam, but it creates the illusion of eye contact for the person on the other end. Lighting also plays a big part in how you're perceived. Aim for a well-lit space, preferably with natural light, as it not only makes you look more awake but also helps avoid the spooky "horror movie" look that overhead lights can create. Adjusting your background to be tidy and non-distracting can help keep the focus on you rather than the pile of laundry lurking in the corner.

Now, let's tackle the auditory side of things. Clear audio is crucial for effective communication, so consider investing in a good microphone or headset. This doesn't mean you need a setup worthy of a professional podcaster—just something that ensures your voice is heard without echoes or background noise. Use a clear, steady voice, and take pauses when needed to let your message sink in. Pauses give others a chance to jump in, making the conversation feel more natural and less like you're delivering a monologue worthy of a Shakespearean play.

Yet, even with the best preparations, video calls are not without their hiccups. Technical issues seem to have a knack for popping up at the worst moments, like when you're about to land that killer punchline in a presentation. To handle these smoothly, ensure your software is updated and do a quick test run before important meetings. If things go awry, stay calm and communicate the issue. Remember, everyone has been there, and a bit of humor can go a long way in smoothing over any awkwardness. Delays and audio lags are other common pitfalls. Don't fill the silence with nervous chatter when it happens; just resist the urge. Instead, pause, let the delay catch up, and then continue.

Quick Video Call Prep Checklist

- Check Your Tech: Ensure your camera and microphone are working.
- Light It Right: Use natural light when possible.
- Tidy Up: Keep your background clean and simple.
- Look at the Lens: Make eye contact by looking at the camera.
- Stay Cool: Have a backup plan for tech hiccups.

Digital conversations can be tricky, but once you've got the right tools, you'll stop fumbling and start actually connecting.

7.1 TEXT-BASED CONVERSATIONS: READING BETWEEN THE LINES

Ah, the world of text messages and emails—where misunderstandings happen as quickly as you can type "LOL." It's a place where you can say "K" and somehow offend your best friend or send a seemingly innocent emoji that gets wildly misinterpreted. Welcome to the digital minefield of text-based communication. Unlike face-to-face chats, these digital conversations lack the richness of vocal tone and body language, making it easy for messages to be misread. Tone and word choice become crucial here. A short response might seem curt or disinterested, while an overly detailed one might appear excessive or even passive-aggressive. Emojis and punctuation step in as the unsung heroes, adding layers of emotion to the otherwise flat text. A smiley face can soften a critique, and an exclamation point can turn a "thanks" into a "thank you so much!" Still, these elements can't fully replicate the nuances of in-person communication, so treading carefully is key.

When crafting your messages, aim for clarity by keeping your language concise. This isn't the time for Shakespearean prose—think more Hemingway. Short, direct sentences ensure your point isn't lost in translation. Balancing formality and informality can also make a big difference. You wouldn't send your boss a text filled with emojis (unless you want to make it onto their "do not promote" list), so adapt your tone according to your audience. Feel free to throw in those LOLs and smiley faces if you're texting a friend. But remember, even with friends, context is everything. A well-placed emoji can lighten the mood, but an overused one might make you look like you have an emoji obsession.

Improving your ability to interpret written communication is a skill worth mastering. Start with text analysis exercises. Take a message you received and break it down. What does the word choice suggest? Are there any hidden meanings or implied emotions? Look for contextual clues that provide insight into the sender's intent. For example, a message sent late at night might carry a different urgency than one sent during the day. Practice with different types of messages—from casual texts to formal emails—and see if you can spot patterns. This exercise not only sharpens your interpretive skills but also helps you become more mindful of how you craft your own messages.

Avoiding misunderstandings in text requires a bit of vigilance. When in doubt, ask clarifying questions. If someone says, "We need to talk," don't start panicking about the state of your friendship. Instead, reply with something like, "Sure, what's up?" This invites them to elaborate and gives you a clearer picture of their intent. Techniques for resolving ambiguity can also be helpful. If a message leaves you scratching your head, try paraphrasing it back to the sender. Say something like, "Just to make sure I'm on the same page, you're saying..." This not only clarifies the message but also shows the other person that you're genuinely trying to understand them.

Navigating text-based communication can feel like walking a tightrope, but with practice, you can become adept at decoding the subtle cues embedded in every message. It's about finding that sweet spot where your words convey exactly what you mean, emojis and all.

7.2 MANAGING MULTITASKING IN DIGITAL COMMUNICATION

So, there you are, trying to follow a virtual meeting while also checking emails and sneaking a peek at social media. Sound familiar? Multitasking, especially in digital settings, can feel like an Olympic sport. You might think you're getting more done, but here's the kicker: multitasking can actually sabotage your listening skills and comprehension. It's like trying to juggle balls while riding a unicycle—something's bound to hit the ground. In virtual environments, this juggling act often involves toggling between screens, responding to messages, and even munching on snacks during meetings. All these distractions can dilute your focus, turning what should be a straightforward conversation into a garbled mess of half-heard ideas and missed cues. The quality of communication suffers, and before you know it, you're nodding along without a clue about what was just discussed. It's not just about missing information; it's about missing the connection that happens when you're truly present.

Reducing digital multitasking isn't about giving up all your devices and going off-grid. It's about creating a workspace that minimizes distractions. Think of it as setting up a zen zone for your mind. Start by getting rid of any unused junk from your workspace—an organized environment can support clearer thinking. Consider using apps that block distracting websites during meetings or work sessions. These digital helpers can keep you focused and make those endless rabbit holes of distraction a thing of the past. Time management is another key player here. Set aside specific times for going through emails or social media, and stick to those windows. This way, you're not constantly pulled away from the task at hand. It's like setting boundaries for your digital life, letting you be fully present when it counts.

Single-tasking might sound outdated in our fast-paced world, but it's one of the most effective ways to improve concentration. Instead of spreading your attention thin, focus on one task at a time. Start with small exercises to build this habit. For instance, set a timer for 15 minutes and dedicate that time solely to the task at hand, whether it's a meeting or a project. Gradually increase the time as your concentration improves. Mindfulness practices tailored for digital contexts can also enhance your focus. Try a quick meditation before a big call, or take a few deep breaths to center yourself. These practices help anchor your attention, ensuring you're fully engaged.

Evaluating your multitasking habits is a crucial step toward improvement. Self-assessment tools can shed light on your tendencies, helping you understand when and why you drift into multitasking mode.

Reflect on your communication effectiveness, too. After a virtual meeting, ask yourself: Did I catch all the key points? Was there anything I missed because I was distracted? Journaling these reflections will help you track patterns and make adjustments. It's about being honest with yourself and recognizing areas for growth. This self-awareness empowers you to make intentional changes, enhancing your listening skills and communication quality.

As we navigate this digital age, embracing a more focused approach can transform how we engage with others. By cutting down on multitasking and honing our ability to concentrate, we open the door to richer, more meaningful interactions.

7.3 CREATING PRESENCE IN VIRTUAL MEETINGS

Ever catch yourself zoning out during a virtual meeting, only to snap back and realize you missed the part where your name was mentioned? You're not alone. Being present in a virtual setting means more than just showing up and nodding occasionally. It's about engaging actively, both mentally and visually. A strong virtual presence is marked by attentiveness and genuine participation, which, let's face it, is trickier over a screen than in person. It involves ensuring you're not just a silent square on someone's screen but an active contributor to the discussion. This presence helps maintain the flow of conversation and ensures that your voice and ideas are heard and valued. Plus, being present can significantly enhance the overall productivity and positivity of the meeting. It's like adding that secret ingredient to a dish that makes everyone go, "Wow, what's in this?"

To project attentiveness and engagement during virtual meetings, maintain eye contact with the camera. Yes, it might feel like you're staring into the void, but to the person on the other side, it looks like you're making direct eye contact. This simple trick can make interactions feel more personal and connected. Add to that a few active listening signals like nodding or giving verbal affirmations such as "I see" or "That makes sense." These cues show the speaker that you're engaged, transforming the virtual space into a more interactive and lively one. It's like being the enthusiastic audience member in a stand-up show who keeps the energy up. And don't forget to keep your body language open and relaxed, much like you would in an in-person meeting, to convey openness and receptivity.

Active participation is key in making your presence felt in virtual meetings. This doesn't mean jumping in at every opportunity to make a point, but it involves meaningfully contributing. Asking insightful questions can demonstrate that you're physically present and mentally engaged with the discussion. It's like adding seasoning to a conversation—a well-placed question can bring out new flavors and insights. Aim to do so when contributing in a way that flows with the conversation rather than interrupting it. This might mean jotting down thoughts and waiting for a natural pause to share them. It's about finding that balance between being heard and allowing others to speak, like a well-conducted orchestra where every instrument has time to shine.

Of course, staying present in virtual meetings isn't without its hurdles. Virtual meeting fatigue is a real thing—those back-to-back meetings can drain anyone's energy. Take regular breaks between meetings to recharge your mental batteries and combat this. A quick walk around the room or a few minutes of stretching can work wonders. If you find your mind wandering during a meeting, try re-engaging by focusing on the speaker's words and summarizing them in your head. This practice can help draw your attention back and keep you grounded in the discussion. Distractions are another common obstacle. Whether it's the allure of checking emails or the siren call of social media, these can pull you away from being present. Create a distraction-free zone by silencing notifications and closing unnecessary tabs, much like locking away the cookie jar to avoid temptation.

Maintaining a presence in virtual meetings is like perfecting a dance routine—you might stumble initially, but with practice, it becomes second nature. It's about finding your rhythm, engaging actively, and navigating the digital dance floor with poise and confidence. So, next time you log in for a meeting, remember that your presence is more than just a click of the "join" button—it's an active choice to engage, contribute, and connect.

7.4 TOOLS AND TECHNOLOGIES FOR ENHANCED DIGITAL LISTENING

In this digital age, technology offers a treasure trove of tools designed to enhance our communication and listening skills. Whether you're navigating a virtual meeting or simply trying to make a deeper connection with friends and family over text, these tools can be game-changers. Consider popular digital listening aids like noise-canceling headphones, which drown out distractions to help you focus on the person you're talking to. Or, how about transcription apps that capture every spoken word, letting you revisit conversations later? Platforms like Otter.ai and Rev offer real-time transcription, ensuring you don't miss a beat. These technologies not only aid in capturing conversations but also provide the flexibility to review and reflect on discussions, enabling you to engage more thoughtfully. When used effectively, they can transform how you interact in the digital space, turning each conversation into a chance for a deeper understanding and connection.

So, picking the right tool for your needs can be like choosing the perfect avocado—sometimes, it's hard to know what you're actually getting until you dig in. But fear not; I've got some criteria to help you evaluate your options. First, consider your specific communication challenges. Are you struggling with hearing clarity on calls, or do you often need to revisit what was said? For those needing clearer audio, a high-quality headset with a built-in microphone is a lifesaver. If it's about comprehension and retention, a transcription service might be just what the doctor ordered. Also, think about the context in which you'll use these tools. A tool perfect for a bustling home office might not fit a quiet library setting best. Use what fits. The right tool, used correctly, can seriously level up how you connect online.

Once you've picked your digital helpers, the challenge will be seam-lessly integrating them into your daily routine. It might take a little while to get used to relying on technology, but with a few best prac-tices, you'll soon find them indispensable. Start with a bit of training and familiarization. Take some time to explore the features of the tool you picked while watching a few tutorial videos. This prep work ensures you're not just using the technology but maximizing its poten-tial. Also, introduce these tools gradually, allowing yourself and your communication partners to adapt comfortably. For instance, if you're using transcription software, let your conversation partner know—it might take some pressure off trying to remember every detail, and they might appreciate the transparency.

Evaluating the effectiveness of these tools isn't a one-and-done task. It requires ongoing reflection and feedback. After using a new tool, seek input from those you communicate with regularly. Ask them if they've noticed any improvements in clarity or engagement. Are your conversations feeling more productive or enjoyable? Use this feedback to make tweaks and adjustments. You may need a different tool, or it's just changing how you use it. Continuous improvement is the name of the game here. Keep an eye on how these technologies impact your listening skills and communication efficiency, and don't hesitate to switch things up if they're not meeting expectations. The goal is to create a dynamic communication environment that evolves with your needs and enhances your ability to connect with others.

Embracing digital tools for communication opens up a world of possibilities. It's like having a Swiss Army knife for your listening skills, with each tool offering a unique way to enhance interaction. But, like any tool, their value comes from how you use them. When you choose the right tools, use them intentionally, and take time to assess what's working, you can really improve the quality of your digital communication. As we close this chapter on digital communication, remember that the right combination of technology and technique can bridge the gap between mere conversation and true connection.

CHAPTER 8
BUILDING CUSTOMIZED LISTENING PLANS

IMAGINE YOU'RE AT A GATHERING, and someone starts telling you about their passion for collecting vintage toasters. You nod politely, but your mind wanders, thinking about that new series you want to binge-watch. Sound familiar? We've all been there. Like any skill, listening can use a little polish now and then. Welcome to the chapter where we dig into the nitty-gritty of your listening habits and challenges. It's time to look in the mirror and figure out what's working, what's not, and how to tweak it all for the better.

8.1 ASSESSING YOUR LISTENING HABITS AND CHALLENGES

Let's start with identifying your current listening patterns. Think of this as a self-audit for your ears. Grab a self-assessment questionnaire (they're everywhere online, and some are even fun) and start jotting down your strengths and weaknesses. Are you a nod-along listener, or do you zone out halfway through a chat? Reflect on past communication experiences and consider moments when you felt like a listening rockstar and others when you were more like a space cadet. These reflections are crucial for pinpointing where you shine and where you might need extra attention. When I did this, I realized I was great at listening to friends vent about their day but terrible at staying engaged during long work meetings.

Once you grasp your habits, it's time to recognize those pesky personal listening challenges. These obstacles pop up like uninvited guests at a party, derailing your focus. Identify the frequent distractions you face. Is it the constant ping of your smartphone, the chatter of colleagues in the background, or even your own wandering thoughts? Recognizing these distractions is the first step toward conquering them. Then, consider the emotional triggers that might be lurking in your conversations. Maybe a certain topic always sets you off, or perhaps a particular tone of voice rubs you the wrong way. Knowing what sets you off makes you more likely to keep your cool and handle it like a pro.

To thoroughly evaluate your listening skills, you need the right tools. Listening-style inventories are a great starting point. They categorize your listening habits and reveal insights about your preferred listening style, whether it's people-oriented, action-oriented, content-oriented, or time-oriented. Additionally, peer feedback mechanisms can provide valuable insights. Try asking a colleague or a friend to give you the hard truth about your listening skills. Sure, it might sting a bit, but constructive criticism is a goldmine for improvement. When I first asked for feedback, I was surprised to learn that I often interrupted without realizing it. Armed with that knowledge, I could work on it.

Once you've gathered all this information, it's time to analyze the assessment results. This is where the magic happens. Think of it as conducting a SWOT analysis—Strengths, Weaknesses, Opportunities, and Threats—of your listening skills. Identify the strengths you can build on, the weaknesses you need to address, the opportunities for growth, and the threats (like distractions and triggers) you need to manage. This analysis is your roadmap for improvement. It highlights the areas where you can make the most significant impact and guides you in creating a customized listening plan that suits your unique needs.

Take a moment to conduct a SWOT analysis of your listening skills. Divide a sheet of paper into four columns and jot down your strengths, weaknesses, opportunities, and threats. Reflect on what you've learned and consider how to use this information to improve your listening.

SWOT Listening Exercise for Your Fasting Journey

This exercise helps you reflect on your **Strengths, Weaknesses, Opportunities, and Threats (SWOT)** in your fasting practice. By understanding these areas, you can make better decisions, stay consistent, and improve your results.

Instructions:

1. Divide a sheet of paper into four sections: **Strengths, Weaknesses, Opportunities, and Threats**.
2. Take time to jot down thoughts in each section.
3. Reflect on what you've learned and identify ways to enhance your fasting experience.

■ STRENGTHS (WHAT'S WORKING?)

Write down what you're doing well in your fasting routine. Consider things like:

Staying consistent with your fasting schedule

Managing hunger effectively

Choosing nutrient-dense foods

Noticing increased energy or focus

Maintaining hydration levels

■ WEAKNESSES (WHAT'S CHALLENGING?)

Identify areas where you struggle. This could be:

Feeling fatigued or sluggish at certain times

Struggling with social situations and food pressure

Breaking fasts with unhealthy choices

Experiencing cravings or emotional eating

Difficulty adjusting fasting hours due to lifestyle

■ OPPORTUNITIES (HOW CAN YOU IMPROVE?)

Look for ways to refine your approach and set yourself up for success:

Experimenting with different fasting windows

Meal prepping to avoid poor food choices

Incorporating mindful eating to enhance digestion

Using tracking tools to monitor progress

Learning more about how fasting impacts your body

THREATS (WHAT COULD DERAIL YOUR PROGRESS?)

Recognize potential obstacles and prepare strategies to overcome them:

Stress or emotional triggers leading to breaking a fast early

Social events that make fasting difficult

Lack of sleep affecting energy levels

Traveling or schedule changes disrupting your routine

Feeling discouraged due to slow progress

Reflection Questions:

1. **What did you learn from this exercise?**
2. **How can your strengths help you navigate or improve areas where you struggle?**
3. **What opportunities will you take advantage of this week?**
4. **How can you plan ahead to manage threats to your fasting success?**

You can fine-tune your fasting routine for long-term success by actively listening to your body and habits. Keep this SWOT analysis as a reference and update it as you progress!

By understanding your current listening habits and challenges, you're laying the foundation for meaningful change. This self-awareness gets you ready to make informed decisions about enhancing your listening skills, ultimately leading to more fulfilling and effective communication.

8.2 SETTING REALISTIC GOALS FOR LISTENING IMPROVEMENT

Ever set a goal so vague that it felt like trying to catch fog? Yeah, me too. Without clear goals, improving your listening skills can feel like spinning in a hamster wheel—you're moving but not getting anywhere. Goals give you direction and purpose. They're like a GPS for your personal development journey, keeping you motivated and on track. Setting specific and achievable goals creates a roadmap for success, and goal-setting becomes a motivator. It's the difference between saying, "I want to be a better listener," and saying, "I want to improve my listening skills by learning to ask clarifying questions during discussions." One feels like a wish, and the other feels like a plan.

Crafting SMART goals is a game-changer in this process. These goals are Specific, Measurable, Achievable, Relevant, and Time-bound. Think of them as your personal blueprint. For instance, if you aim to reduce distractions during conversations, a SMART goal might look like this: "I will minimize phone distractions by keeping my phone in another room during dinner conversations for two weeks." It's specific because it targets phone distractions, measurable because you can track for two weeks, achievable because it's within your control, relevant to your listening improvement, and time-bound with a clear deadline. This framework transforms abstract desires into concrete steps, making seeing progress and staying motivated easier.

Now, aligning these goals with your personal and professional needs is important. You don't want to end up with goals that feel disconnected from your life. Take a moment to identify your personal communication priorities. Maybe you're focused on improving family dynamics or enhancing professional relationships. Align your listening goals with these priorities to ensure they resonate with your day-to-day life. For example, to advance your career, target goals like enhancing active listening in team meetings or improving feedback reception. These tailored goals elevate your listening skills and support your broader aspirations, harmonizing personal growth and career objectives.

Creating a goal-tracking system is the secret sauce to staying on course. Without it, goals can easily slip through the cracks of daily life. Start by using goal-tracking templates that suit your style. It could be a journal where you jot down daily reflections or a digital app that sends reminders. The key is consistency. Regularly review your progress, weekly or monthly, to assess how far you've come and what adjustments are needed. These review sessions are your chance to celebrate victories, no matter how small, and recalibrate if necessary. They keep you accountable, ensuring that your goals remain a priority and that you're continuously moving toward becoming the listener you aspire to be.

Setting realistic goals for listening improvement is akin to plotting a course for an exciting adventure. These goals anchor you, keeping you focused and motivated, while the SMART framework provides the structure to ensure success. You create a holistic approach to growth that enriches every facet of your life by aligning your goals with your personal and professional goals. With a solid goal-tracking system, you will be ready to monitor your progress, enjoy your achievements, and make any necessary adjustments. So, grab your pen, jot down those goals, and start plotting your course toward becoming the listener you've always wanted to be.

8.3 TAILORING TECHNIQUES TO YOUR UNIQUE NEEDS

So, you've got your listening goals sorted. Now, it's time to tweak those techniques to fit like your favorite pair of jeans—comfortable and oh-so-right. Listening isn't a one-size-fits-all gig, so let's personalize those strategies to suit your needs. Start by customizing mindfulness practices. Maybe you find traditional meditation about as exciting as watching paint dry. No problem. How about trying a walking meditation where you focus on the sights and sounds around you? Or even a mindful coffee break, savoring each sip like a mini-vacation? The key is to find what makes mindfulness feel natural for you, not something forced or awkward.

Adjusting empathy exercises is another place to get creative. Consider alternative ways to engage if role-playing scenarios feel too much like an awkward high school drama class. You could try empathy mapping, drawing out someone's experiences and emotions like a treasure map. Or perhaps keep an empathy journal, jotting down moments when you felt truly connected with someone else's feelings. By tailoring these exercises, you make empathy a habit, not a chore, and soon, you'll find it slipping into your conversations like a ninja—quietly but oh-so-effectively.

Incorporating feedback is the secret sauce in personalizing your listening techniques. It's like having a backstage pass to your own performance, with your peers playing the role of the critics. Seek constructive criticism from those who've seen you in action. Ask a friend if you monopolize conversations or frequently interrupt. Be ready for honesty, and remember, this isn't about getting a pat on the back—it's about growth. Use their suggestions as a springboard for improvement. Maybe they'll suggest you pause more often or ask clarifying questions. Implement these tweaks and watch your listening skills evolve into something more impactful, like upgrading from a black-and-white movie to full Technicolor.

Balancing different listening approaches can feel like juggling flaming torches while riding a unicycle. But fear not; it's all about finding your rhythm and combining analytical listening, which focuses on details and facts, with empathic listening, which hones in on emotions and feelings. Consider a hybrid approach, where you start by understanding the content and then shift to understanding the context and emotions behind it. And let's not forget nonverbal communication strategies. Integrate them into your routine, like maintaining eye contact, nodding at key points, and mirroring the speaker's gestures. It's about creating a medley of techniques that work for you, allowing you to switch gears seamlessly based on the conversation.

Documenting your personalized techniques is crucial to maintaining and enhancing your listening prowess. Think of it as building a personal listening toolkit—a collection of strategies you can whip out when needed. Keep a dedicated notebook or digital document where you jot down what works and what doesn't, much like a chef's recipe book. Record your favorite mindfulness practices, empathy exercises, and feedback-driven improvements. This toolkit becomes your go-to resource, ensuring you can tackle any listening scenario. Plus, it's a great way to track your progress, reminding you of how far you've come on this listening adventure.

8.4 CREATING A SUPPORTIVE ENVIRONMENT FOR PRACTICE

Ever tried to read a book at a rock concert? Yeah, it's not the ideal setting for concentration. Like practicing listening skills requires an environment that supports focus and minimizes distractions. Imagine your listening practice setting as a cozy nook designed to block out the world's noise. Start with the basics: seating and acoustics. Choose a comfortable chair that encourages alertness, not a couch that will have you dozing off in seconds. Arrange your space to minimize echoes or background noise—soft furnishings like rugs and cushions can work wonders. Think of your practice area as a soundproof cocoon where your ears are the stars. Visual aids and reminders, like sticky notes with key listening tips or inspiring quotes, can also help keep you on track. It's like having your personal cheerleading squad urging you on.

The space around you matters—but so do the people in it. Being around those who value growth and connection can have a powerful impact on how you listen and engage. Encourage family and colleagues to join you on this listening adventure. Not only will this create a shared experience, but it's also a chance to practice in different settings. Imagine family dinners where everyone commits to listening without interruptions or work meetings where colleagues give feedback on listening improvements. Networking with fellow learners can be another game-changer. Find your people—online or in person. Being around others chasing the same goals keeps you fired up and gives you fresh ways to think. You might even pick up new techniques along the way, like collecting trading cards, but for skills.

Now, let's talk tech. In this digital age, technology isn't just for binge-watching shows or ordering takeout; it's a valuable ally in your listening practice. Consider apps designed for focus and mindfulness.

These handy tools can guide you through exercises that boost your concentration and help keep you in the moment. Apps like Headspace or Calm offer guided meditations that can sharpen your mindfulness, making it easier to tune into conversations. Don't underestimate the power of online communities, either. Platforms like Reddit or specialized listening forums are filled with people sharing tips, experiences, and encouragement. It's like having a global support group at your fingertips.

Technology can also provide great tools for feedback and reflection. Some apps allow you to record conversations (with permission, of course) so you can listen back and identify areas for improvement. It's like having a mirror for your listening skills, reflecting back on what you might have missed in the moment. And let's not forget the power of podcasts. Tuning into shows that focus on communication and listening can provide both inspiration and practical advice—it's learning on the go, perfect for those morning commutes or afternoon jogs.

Creating a supportive environment for your listening practice isn't just about removing distractions; it's about cultivating a physical and social space that encourages growth and engagement. Whether you rearrange your living room, set up a cozy listening nook, or embrace digital tools, every little change can make a big difference.

8.5 MONITORING PROGRESS AND ADJUSTING PLANS

Picture yourself at the gym, working up a sweat. You wouldn't spend weeks lifting weights without checking your progress, right? The same concept applies to listening skills. Regular progress evaluation is your fitness tracker in the world of personal development. It's vital to set aside time to assess how you're doing. Think of scheduling regular evaluation sessions as a way to keep yourself accountable. Whether every week or month, mark it on your calendar like a meeting with a friend you want to see. During these sessions, reflect on your recent conversations and interactions. Ask yourself: Have I been more attentive? Did I catch those nonverbal cues? It's not just about ticking boxes;

it's about seeing where you've improved and where you need more work.

Sometimes, sticking to a plan is like trying to stick a square peg into a round hole. That's where adapting plans based on feedback becomes crucial. Flexibility is your best friend here. If you've received constructive feedback from peers or noticed areas that need tweaking, don't fret. Implementing changes is like adjusting the sails on a boat—it keeps you moving forward, even if the wind changes direction. Maybe your friend mentioned you tend to interrupt when excited. Take that in stride and practice pausing before responding. Adjust your techniques as needed, and remember, it's okay to make mistakes. They're like little learning detours that guide you back on track.

Now, let's talk about setbacks. They're the unwelcome guests at the party of progress. But fear not, because overcoming setbacks is entirely doable with the right mindset. Start by recognizing that plateaus are normal. Everyone hits them, and they're not a sign of failure. They're just a signal to shake things up. Try new listening techniques or revisit old ones with a fresh perspective. Sometimes, reigniting motivation is as simple as revisiting why you started this listening improvement adventure in the first place. Reflect on moments when your improved listening made a difference, whether a heartfelt conversation with a loved one or a productive meeting at work. These reflections are like kindling for your fire, keeping your motivation burning bright.

Also, don't forget to celebrate and enjoy your wins. Progress, no matter how small, deserves recognition. Celebrating achievements and milestones is not just about popping champagne—it's about acknowledging your hard work and dedication to becoming a better listener. Set specific milestone celebrations, like having a nice dinner or enjoying a relaxing weekend getaway. Reflect on your growth and achievements, and take a moment to feel proud of how far you've come. These celebrations fuel the journey ahead, reminding you that you're on the right path and capable of incredible things. So, give yourself a pat on the back, do a little happy dance, and keep pushing forward.

As you monitor your progress and make necessary tweaks, remember that this is all part of the bigger picture—becoming a more engaged, empathetic, and effective communicator. With every step, you're not just improving your listening skills; you're enhancing your personal and professional relationships. As you continue this journey, the next chapter awaits, ready to dive deeper into the world of advanced listening techniques.

CHAPTER 9
EXPERT INSIGHTS AND REAL-LIFE APPLICATIONS

IMAGINE you're at a dinner party, and you're introduced to someone with the uncanny ability to make everyone feel like the most important person in the room. It's as if they have a magical power to listen so intently that you wonder if they have superhuman hearing. Well, they're not superheroes, but they're pretty close. These are the communication experts whose insights have transformed how we understand and practice listening. Their wisdom is like a treasure map leading us to uncover the hidden gems of effective communication. Let's dive into their world and see what we can learn.

Meet Julian Treasure, a name you might recognize from his viral TED Talks about the power of sound and listening. Julian is a renowned author and sound expert who has spent years studying how sound affects us. His work emphasizes the importance of conscious listening and how it shapes our interactions. Then there's Dr. Brené Brown, a research professor and storyteller whose work on vulnerability and empathy has captured the hearts of millions. Her insights into the power of connection have redefined how we approach conversations. And let's not forget Marshall Rosenberg, the creator of Nonviolent Communication (NVC), whose methods have guided countless individuals in navigating tricky dialogues with grace and understanding.

These experts have laid down some golden rules for effective listening. One of the standout principles is "active silence," a concept that sounds like an oxymoron but is anything but. Active silence is about being fully present in a conversation without jumping in to fill every pause. It's the art of letting the silence speak, giving space for thoughts to settle and insights to emerge. Then there's "empathetic engagement," which goes beyond just hearing words. It's about diving into the emotional undercurrents of a conversation, understanding the feelings behind the words, and responding with genuine empathy.

Now, let's talk strategy. Julian Treasure often speaks about "deep listening," a practice that involves tuning in not just to the words but also to the tone, pitch, and rhythm of what's being said. It's like listening to music and catching the subtle harmonies that make the piece come alive. Brené Brown champions the concept of "constructive feedback loops," where feedback is given and received in a manner that promotes growth and solidifies relationships. It's about making a cycle of positive reinforcement a place where both parties feel heard and valued.

But how do you incorporate these expert insights into your daily life without feeling overwhelmed? Start with small exercises inspired by their methodologies. resisting the urge to interrupt during conversations by practicing "active silence." Let the other person finish their thoughts entirely before you respond. For "deep listening," try focusing on the speaker's vocal nuances. Notice the rise and fall of their voice and what it might indicate about their emotions. As for "empathetic engagement," challenge yourself to paraphrase what you've heard to confirm your understanding and show that you've truly absorbed the essence of the message.

Reflection Exercise: Expert Listening Insights

Take a moment to reflect on your recent conversations. Did you practice active silence, deep listening, or empathetic engagement? Write down your observations and any changes you noticed in the quality of the interactions. How did these techniques impact your understanding and connection with the speaker?

Incorporating these expert insights into your listening practices can transform your communication skills. It's about being intentional, present, and open to the myriad ways people express themselves. As you continue to explore the landscape of listening, remember that these small shifts can lead to monumental changes in how you connect with the world around you.

9.1 REAL-LIFE CASE STUDIES: SUCCESS STORIES IN LISTENING

Let's talk about case studies for a moment. They're like the behind-the-scenes footage of real-world listening triumphs. You get to see the messy bits, the aha moments, and everything in between. They offer a glimpse into how listening can transform situations that seemed doomed from the start. It's like watching a sports game where the underdog team pulls off a last-minute win—only here, the victory is in understanding and connection.

Take this corporate scenario, for instance. A team at a mid-sized tech company was struggling. Their meetings were chaotic, with overlapping voices and ideas lost in the noise. Frustration was high, and so was tension. They decided to try something radical: implement structured listening techniques. The team began using talking sticks—a simple but effective tool. Whoever held the stick got to speak, and everyone else had to listen. It sounds elementary, but it was a game-changer. Suddenly, ideas flowed smoothly, and members felt respected and heard. The results? Project timelines improved, creativity soared, and the team dynamics shifted from disjointed to harmonious.

Let's shift gears to something more personal. Picture a couple who'd been married for years yet found themselves speaking different languages—or so it seemed. Miscommunications had crept into their daily lives like uninvited guests. They were at a crossroads, uncertain how to bridge the emotional gap. Enter active listening. They started small, dedicating time each evening to fully focus on each other's words without distractions. They practiced reflecting on each other's feelings, not just the words. It wasn't easy at first, but their communication began to transform as the weeks passed. They rediscovered empathy and understanding, reigniting a sense of partnership that had been buried under years of routine.

What made these transformations possible? Empathy and trust played starring roles in both scenarios. Empathy allowed team members and the couple to see beyond words, connecting on a deeper level. Trust, once established, created a safe space for honest communication. Consistent practice was the backbone of their success. It wasn't a one-off effort but a commitment to change, day by day. The structured listening tools became part of the team's DNA in the corporate setting. Meanwhile, the couple's evening conversations became a cherished ritual, reinforcing the bond they once thought was fading.

These stories highlight the ripple effect that genuine listening can have. Although the initial challenges seemed insurmountable, they discovered new paths forward through focused listening and a willingness to adapt. This is a testament to the power of listening—not just as a skill but as a catalyst for change.

9.2 OVERCOMING PROFESSIONAL LISTENING CHALLENGES

Navigating the workplace is like trying to steer a ship through stormy seas. Cross-departmental misunderstandings are lurking below the surface, waiting to trip you up. It's the classic game of telephone, where a simple request for "more coffee" ends up as "launch a new brand of coffee." The root of these misunderstandings often lies in the lack of effective listening. Departments have their own jargon, timelines, and priorities, creating silos that make communication as clear as mud. Hierarchical barriers can also stifle open dialogue. Picture this: You're in a meeting, and the CEO has spoken. Suddenly, there's a collective nodding of heads, even if half the room is wondering what was just said. People hesitate to ask questions or challenge ideas due to the fear of ruffling feathers.

So, how do we tackle these professional listening obstacles? Let's start with meetings, which can be a productivity powerhouse or a time-sucking black hole. Enter the world of active listening techniques. These involve focusing entirely on the speaker, observing nonverbal cues, and reflecting on what's been said to confirm understanding. It's about being present and genuinely engaged. In virtual team settings, managing communications requires more finesse. With everyone scattered across different locations, it's easy for messages to get lost in the digital ether. Encourage the use of video when possible, which brings back some of those nonverbal cues. Set clear agendas and assign roles to keep the chaos in check. And don't forget to follow up with summaries to ensure everyone is on the same page.

Let's look at a scenario where a project collaboration faced serious roadblocks to see these strategies in action. Teams from marketing and product development were at odds. Meetings often ended in confusion, with both sides feeling unheard. They decided to implement structured listening techniques, starting with dedicated listening sessions. During these sessions, each team could present their perspectives without interruption. The results were impressive. Misunderstandings decreased, ideas flowed more freely, and the project timeline improved. Then, there's the case of client communication. A sales team struggling with client retention rates decided to focus on active listening during client interactions. They asked open-ended questions, listened without interrupting, and used paraphrasing to ensure they captured the clients' needs accurately. The outcome? Client satisfaction soared, and retention rates followed suit.

Feedback from professionals who have embraced these listening strategies often reads like a success story. One workplace leader noted how structured listening transformed their team dynamics, increasing productivity and morale. Another team member shared how active listening helped them feel more valued and engaged in meetings. When people feel heard, they're more likely to contribute and collaborate effectively. These testimonials highlight the transformative power of listening—it's like discovering a secret ingredient that elevates the whole dish.

Listening in the workplace isn't just about avoiding misunderstandings or ticking a box on the "good employee" checklist. It's about making a place where ideas can grow and feedback is given and received gracefully. It breeds a culture of openness and trust, so everyone can feel empowered to speak up and share their thoughts. So, remember that listening is your superpower the next time you're in a meeting or engaging with a colleague. It could turn the stormy seas of workplace communication into calm waters where collaboration and innovation can thrive.

9.3 APPLYING ACTIVE LISTENING IN CONFLICT RESOLUTION

Picture this: you're at the family holiday dinner, and the conversation has veered into territory as dangerous as a minefield—politics. Tensions are rising faster than your uncle's blood pressure, and you can almost feel the walls closing in. Enter active listening, your new best friend in these moments. When tempers flare, listening can be the secret sauce that de-escalates the tension and brings everyone back to a place of understanding. It's like an emotional reset button. By focusing on what the other person is saying without immediately jumping in with your own rebuttal, you create a space where emotions can simmer down rather than boil over. This approach isn't just about staying quiet. It's about truly engaging with the other person's perspective, even if it differs wildly from your own. In doing so, you not only reduce the heat of the moment but also pave the way for resolving the conflict altogether.

So, how do you put this into practice when it feels like everyone's ready to grab their pitchforks? Start with maintaining neutrality. That doesn't mean you turn into a robot devoid of opinions; instead, you listen without jumping to conclusions. Picture yourself as a curious detective trying to understand the whole story. Avoid taking sides or letting your emotions dictate your responses. Instead, focus on the facts and the feelings behind them. Next, work on validating opposing viewpoints. This doesn't mean you have to agree with the other person, but showing that you understand their perspective can work wonders. Say things like, "I see why you might feel that way," or "I can understand where you're coming from." These simple affirmations can go a long way in making the other person feel heard and respected, which is often half the battle won.

Let's peek into a real-world example. The workplace was on the brink of chaos. Two departments were at loggerheads over resource allocation, each convinced they were in the right. Meetings turned into shouting matches, and productivity was tanking. Management decided enough was enough and brought in a mediator to facilitate active listening sessions. Each team got a chance to express their concerns while the other listened—really listened. By the end of the process, both sides understood each other's constraints and came to a compromise that satisfied everyone. It's similar to watching a soap opera where everyone gets along in the end, but it wasn't magic—just effective listening.

On the personal front, consider a couple going through a rough patch. Misunderstandings and assumptions had built walls between them that seemed insurmountable. They decided to try something new: dedicate time each week to focus solely on listening to each other without jumping in to defend or explain. Over time, they discovered hidden fears and unspoken desires that had been fueling their arguments. By practicing active listening, they began rebuilding trust and understanding, and the relationship that once felt like a sinking ship started to feel more like a sturdy lifeboat.

But how do you know if your listening efforts are paying off? Look for indicators of successful resolution. Have tensions decreased? Are both parties more willing to engage in dialogue without defensiveness? Consider feedback from the involved parties, asking them how they felt during the process. Did they feel heard and respected? These signs can be your guideposts, showing you're on the right track.

9.4 INSIGHTS FROM THERAPEUTIC LISTENING PRACTICES

Therapeutic listening might sound like something only for therapy rooms with leather couches and soothing music, but hold your horses. This practice fosters healing and understanding through intentional listening, making it valuable beyond just therapy. In a therapeutic setting, listening goes beyond mere words. It is geared toward creating a safe space where individuals feel comfortable opening up, knowing they are heard without judgment. The goal isn't to fix but to understand and support. Therapists often employ reflective listening, a technique where they mirror the speaker's feelings and words, helping the individual hear their own thoughts, sometimes for the first time. It's like holding up a mirror that reflects emotions back to the speaker, allowing them to gain clarity.

Creating a safe listening space requires more than just nodding along. It involves setting the stage for open communication, where the listener's body language, eye contact, and even the silence between words play a crucial role. Therapists are masters of this craft. They know how to maintain an atmosphere where trust can flourish and vulnerability is embraced. This environment encourages individuals to explore their thoughts and feelings without fear of ridicule or dismissal. Reflective listening practices are central to this approach, validating the speaker's experience and making them feel understood and valued.

Consider the case of a young man struggling to express his emotions. He found himself at odds with the world in therapy, feeling unheard and frustrated. Through therapeutic listening, his therapist used reflective listening to acknowledge his feelings without judgment. As the sessions progressed, the young man began to articulate his thoughts more clearly. The simple act of being genuinely listened to allowed him to overcome communication barriers and find his voice. Another example involves a woman dealing with grief. Her therapist used therapeutic listening to help her process her emotions, leading to emotional healing over time. These cases highlight how therapeutic listening can facilitate breakthroughs that seem out of reach.

But here's the kicker: you don't need to be a therapist to harness the power of therapeutic listening. These techniques can be adapted for everyday interactions, enhancing personal and professional communication. Imagine using reflective listening during a conversation with a friend who is having a tough time. By mirroring their emotions and acknowledging their feelings, you provide support and understanding that can strengthen your bond. Creating a safe listening space in the workplace can lead to better teamwork and problem-solving. When team members feel heard, they're more willing to contribute ideas and engage in open dialogue.

The benefits of therapeutic listening extend beyond therapy rooms. It's about fostering connections, promoting understanding, and creating an environment where individuals feel valued. Whether you're supporting a friend, engaging with a colleague, or simply listening to a loved one, incorporating therapeutic listening into your interactions can deepen relationships and enhance communication. It's like adding an extra layer of empathy and understanding to your conversations, making them richer and more meaningful. So, next time you find yourself in a conversation, remember that therapeutic listening is a tool you can use to make a real difference.

As we wrap up this chapter, remember that listening is more than just a skill—it's a way of being present, understanding, and connecting with others. Whether you're using insights from experts or therapeutic techniques in everyday life, listening has the power to transform relationships and foster growth. The next chapter will explore how these listening skills can lead to lifelong learning and personal development, setting the stage for continued growth and understanding.

CHAPTER 10
LIFELONG LEARNING AND REFLECTIVE PRACTICE

IMAGINE you're at a very busy coffee shop, trying to order your usual latte, but the chatter around you drowns out the barista's voice. It's a perfect metaphor for listening in our chaotic world—amidst the noise, really hearing someone can be a challenge. Yet, just like you eventually learn to lip-read your favorite barista's orders, honing your listening skills is a journey that doesn't end. It's a lifelong adventure filled with twists, turns, and the occasional caffeine-fueled detour.

You might be thinking, "Why should I keep working on my listening skills? I've been doing this since I learned to talk!" But here's the kicker: communication styles are evolving faster than the latest TikTok trend. What worked yesterday might not work today. Continuous learning isn't just about keeping up; it's about staying relevant, adaptable, and open to new ways of connecting with others. When you commit to lifelong learning, you open the door to a world of possibilities. You enhance your skills, boost your confidence, and become someone everyone wants to talk to at the next family gathering.

Lifelong learning isn't just some fancy buzzword; it's a way of life. It's about embracing change, adapting to new communication styles, and growing as a person. Take, for example, the shift from face-to-face meetings to virtual calls. Some of us had to learn to read facial expressions through pixelated screens, while others had to master the art of muting themselves before the dog started barking. Adapting to these changes isn't just about keeping up with technology; it's about understanding the nuances of new communication methods and staying connected in meaningful ways.

However, the benefits of lifelong learning go beyond keeping up with change. It fosters personal growth, enhancing skills crucial for personal and professional relationships. When you stay hungry to learn, you become more flexible, challenging, and open to fresh ideas. You sharpen your thinking, solve problems faster—and yeah, crushing a new skill feels pretty damn good. You might even find yourself striking up a conversation with that elusive barista, finally understanding their order without the need for subtitles.

How do you make learning a regular part of your day without it becoming a burden? Begin by carving out intentional time for it, just like any other important task. Think of it as a mini-vacation for your brain—time to unwind, explore, and discover new things. Consistency is key, whether an hour a week or just ten minutes a day. Plus, with the huge array of online courses and workshops available, you can tailor your learning journey to your interests and schedule. From podcasts to webinars, there's something for everyone. You might even find yourself developing a new passion or two along the way.

A growth mindset is your best friend on this lifelong learning adventure. It's the belief that you can always learn, change, and improve. A growth mindset shifts your perspective—challenges become opportunities to learn, and setbacks become part of the path toward success. Encouraging curiosity and exploration opens the door to new experiences and perspectives. You become a lifelong learner, always eager to discover the next chapter in your journey.

One of the greatest resources for continued education is the wealth of books and podcasts available. From bestsellers to hidden gems, there's no shortage of material to fuel your learning journey. Online platforms like Coursera, Udemy, and LinkedIn Learning offer courses on effective communication and advanced listening skills. You can access a world of knowledge at your fingertips with just some quick clicks. And let's not forget the power of community—joining online forums and groups can provide support, feedback, and inspiration as you continue to grow.

Your Listening Learning Toolkit

1. Books: Dive into classics like "The 7 Habits of Highly Effective People" by Stephen Covey or "Crucial Conversations" by Patterson, Grenny, McMillan, and Switzler. These books offer practical insights and strategies to enhance your listening skills.
2. Podcasts: Tune in to shows like "The Listening Lounge" or "Hidden Brain" for engaging discussions and expert advice on improving communication and listening.
3. Online Courses: Explore platforms like Coursera, Udemy, and LinkedIn Learning for courses on active listening, communication strategies, and emotional intelligence.
4. Community: Join a few forums and groups online to share experiences, gain feedback, and connect with fellow learners. Websites like Reddit and Facebook offer communities focused on personal development and communication skills.
5. Journaling: Keep a journal to document your learning journey, reflections, and insights. This practice encourages self-awareness and helps track progress.

Lifelong learning isn't just about accumulating knowledge; it's about transforming how you interact with the world. It's the key to unlocking your full potential, fostering meaningful connections, and staying curious. Whether you're learning to read the subtle cues of a Zoom call or mastering the art of active listening, each step forward enriches your life.

10.1 REFLECTIVE PRACTICE: LEARNING FROM EVERY INTERACTION

Imagine sitting on your porch with a hot cup of coffee, watching the sun dip below the horizon. It's the perfect time to let your mind wander back over the day's conversations. Reflective practice is just that—it's taking a moment to think about what happened, what went well, and what could've gone better. It's about learning from your daily interactions, much like an athlete reviews their performance after a game. This kind of reflection isn't just navel-gazing; it's a powerful tool for refining your listening skills. When you reflect, you notice patterns you might otherwise miss, like how you always interrupt when you're excited or how you sometimes zone out when the topic doesn't interest you. It's about looking at those moments not as failures but as opportunities to improve.

Think of reflection as the polishing cloth for your listening skills. Just as a sculptor refines their work, reflection allows you to hone your ability to truly listen. For instance, maybe you had a conversation with a friend where you realized afterward that you weren't as present as you could've been. Reflecting on that interaction helps you identify why—perhaps you were preoccupied with a work deadline—and allows you to strategize ways to keep similar distractions at bay in the future. By regularly practicing reflection, you gradually become more self-aware and better equipped to handle future conversations with greater presence and empathy.

How do you reflect effectively without turning it into a drawn-out therapy session? One of the most practical tools is keeping a reflection journal. It's like a diary, but you're jotting down notes about your interactions instead of chronicling your life. What was the conversation about? How did it make you feel? What did you notice about your listening? You don't need to write a novel—a few lines will do. If journaling feels too formal, consider structured reflection exercises. After each significant conversation, these might involve asking yourself a series of questions: What did I learn? What could I have done differently? How did my responses affect the other person?

Integrating reflection into your daily routine doesn't have to be a chore. Start small, like a morning ritual with your first cup of coffee or an evening wind-down before bed. Imagine it as a quick mental check-in, asking yourself, "How did my listening go today?" You might use reflection prompts to guide your thoughts, like "What was my best listening moment today?" or "When did I feel disconnected?" These questions make you stop and think—not just about *how* you listen, but what's going on in your head and heart while you do it. That's where the real insight kicks in.

As you make reflection a regular practice, you'll want to measure how it's impacting your listening skills. Look for indicators of reflective growth, like noticing when you become more aware of your tendencies to interrupt or when you catch yourself before zoning out. You might also seek feedback from peers. Ask them if they've noticed changes in your listening. Do they feel more heard, more understood? A fresh set of eyes can help you spot how much you've grown. You're not chasing perfection here—you're just getting better, one win at a time.

Reflective practice is like a backstage pass to your own mind. It allows you to step back, observe, and better understand yourself. It's about identifying your strengths and weaknesses and embracing them as part of your journey. Seeing where you excel and where you falter gives you the power to change. It's like having a personal growth GPS, helping you navigate the complexities of human interaction.

10.2 THE FUTURE OF LISTENING: ADAPTING TO CHANGE

Picture this: you're trying to keep up with a conversation. At the same time, your smartwatch buzzes with notifications, your smart speaker chimes in with a weather update, and your virtual assistant suggests a playlist. It's like juggling flaming torches while riding a unicycle. Welcome to the future, where communication is evolving at lightning speed, and listening needs to keep pace. With technology advancing faster than a toddler on a sugar high, our listening skills must adapt to these changes. Online connections are everywhere, but if you want to really *listen* in the digital world, you must approach it differently.

Technology has transformed how we communicate. From video calls to voice-activated devices, the landscape of interaction is constantly shifting. For example, consider the impact of virtual reality (VR) on communication. VR is no longer limited to gaming—it's making its way into offices, classrooms, and even social spaces. Picture joining a virtual boardroom meeting where your avatar reacts as if you're really there.

Sounds futuristic, doesn't it? But it's happening. In these immersive environments, listening involves more than just ears; it requires reading digital body language and interpreting virtual cues. It's like learning a new language, where a nod has a different weight than a smile emoji.

Cultural trends are also shifting, influencing how we communicate and, by extension, how we listen. As societies become more interconnected, we're exposed to a rich tapestry of cultural expressions. This diversity is a beautiful thing, but it also requires us to be more attuned to nuances in communication. Listening goes beyond words; it involves understanding context, tone, and intent. Imagine interpreting a message from someone whose cultural norms differ from yours. It's like decoding a foreign film without subtitles. Flexibility and openness to diverse cultural expressions become invaluable assets. They enable us to bridge gaps and connect authentically with people from all walks of life.

Adapting our listening skills to new contexts involves embracing change with curiosity instead of hesitation. Start by dipping your toes into the digital pool. Explore new communication platforms, whether a social media app is gaining popularity or a tool like Zoom, which has become a staple in our lives. Familiarize yourself with their features and quirks. It's like learning to dance in a new style—awkward at first, but with practice, it becomes second nature. Stay open to experimenting with different modes of communication. Try sending voice notes instead of texts or engaging in a video call rather than an email exchange. These small changes can diversify your communication toolkit.

The emergence of new communication platforms is inevitable, and preparing for their integration is a proactive step. Social media trends shift like the wind, with platforms appearing and disappearing faster than fashion fads. Staying informed about these trends ensures you're not left in the digital dust. Tech like VR and AR is picking up fast—and it's starting to change how we hang out, learn, and talk, mixing real life with digital in some wild ways. Imagine attending a concert from your living room, surrounded by a virtual crowd. These innovations are not just cool gadgets; they are communication tools that require a new level of listening.

Continuous skill adaptation is key to thriving in this ever-changing landscape. Embrace innovation in your listening practices. Try incorporating new techniques and technologies into your routine. Use a smart speaker to read news updates or engage in language exchange apps to practice understanding diverse accents. As you explore, remain committed to ongoing skill assessment and adaptation. Regularly evaluate your listening abilities and seek feedback from those around you. It's like tuning a musical instrument—small adjustments can make a world of difference in how harmonious your interactions become.

This chapter isn't just about preparing for the future. It's about staying present and adaptable in a world that won't stop moving. Listening isn't static; it's a dynamic, evolving skill that grows with us. As new technologies emerge and cultures intertwine, our ability to listen becomes more vital than ever. Embrace change, explore new possibilities, and keep refining your skills. Because in this fast-paced world, being a great listener is like having a superpower that connects us, enriches our lives, and ensures we're never out of touch with what's important.

As we wrap up this exploration of listening's future, consider how these insights can shape your approach to communication. The path forward is exciting and challenging, with technology and culture constantly changing. Embrace the change, adapt your listening skills, and stay ready for whatever comes next.

CONCLUSION

So here we are—the end of the ride. It's been fun and eye-opening and probably made you rethink a few habits. But this isn't goodbye. It's just the kickoff to being a better listener, communicator, and maybe an even better human—one conversation at a time.

Throughout this book, we've explored the transformative power of active listening. It's about understanding emotions, building empathy, and connecting with others on a deeper level, and not just about hearing words. We've discovered that by tuning into our own emotions and those of others, we can navigate even the most challenging conversations with grace and understanding.

Remember when we talked about the importance of empathy and emotional intelligence? Those aren't just buzzwords—they're the foundation of effective communication. Putting ourselves in someone else's shoes and trying to understand their perspective opens the door to more meaningful relationships and successful collaborations.

We've also learned that active listening isn't a one-size-fits-all approach. It requires adapting to different contexts, whether a one-on-one conversation, a group meeting, or a virtual interaction. By staying flexible and attuned to others' needs, we can ensure that our listening skills are always on point.

But here's the kicker: improving your listening skills isn't a destination; it's a journey. It's about consistently applying what you've learned and making a conscious effort to be more present and engaged in every interaction. Sure, there might be some bumps along the way, but that's all part of the growth process.

So, what's next? Well, it's time to put all this knowledge into action! Start by setting some listening goals for yourself. It could be practicing empathy in daily conversations or staying focused during virtual meetings. Whatever it is, make a plan and hold yourself accountable.

But don't stop there. Make reflection a regular part of your routine. After each significant conversation or interaction, take a moment to think about what went well and what you could improve. Did you find yourself getting distracted? Did you miss an opportunity to show empathy? Use these insights to keep refining your skills.

And remember, the world of communication is always evolving. New technologies and cultural trends will continue to shape how we interact. But by staying curious and open to learning, you'll be well-equipped to adapt and thrive in any context.

I'm right there with you on this journey. I'm constantly working on my listening skills and have much more to learn. But that's the beauty of it —we're all works in progress, and every interaction is an opportunity to grow.

Thank you for joining me on this adventure. Your commitment to becoming a better listener is truly inspiring. Keep practicing, reflect, and, most importantly, connect with others. At the end of the day, that's all about building relationships, one conversation at a time.

I'll leave you with this thought from author and activist Bryant McGill: "One of the most sincere forms of respect is listening to what another has to say." So, go out there and show the world what respectful, empathetic listening looks like. Trust me, it'll make a difference.

Here's to a lifetime of meaningful conversations and powerful connections!

KEEP THE CONVERSATION GOING

So, you made it to the end. You've got the tools. You've practiced the pause. You've stopped bulldozing your way through every conversation (or at least you're trying). Now what?

Now it's your turn to help someone else start.

Dropping a quick review on Amazon doesn't just make my day—it helps another curious human out there find this book. And if it helped you, chances are it'll help someone else too.

Maybe they're a burned-out manager.

Maybe they're someone who never felt heard and wants to change that.

Maybe they just need a little nudge to start listening like they mean it.

Whatever their reason, **your words might be the reason they take the first step.**

Your review doesn't have to be fancy:

- Did this book help you *get it* in a way others didn't?
- Did you catch yourself mid-interruption and finally shut up? (Nice!)
- Did something finally click that you wish you knew years ago?

Say that. Say it however you want. Just be real.

Click, Scan or Copy link below to leave your review on Amazon:

[https://www.amazon.com/review/review-your-purchases/?asin= BOOKASIN]

Thanks for being here. Thanks for listening. And thanks for keeping the message alive.

– JD Vaughn

REFERENCES

- *Empathy: A Cornerstone of Effective Communication and ...* https://everydayspeech.com/blog-posts/general/empathy-a-cornerstone-of-effective-communication-and-connection/
- *Using Emotional Intelligence to Improve Communication* https://www.ddiworld.com/blog/emotional-intelligence-and-communication
- *How to Practice Mindful Listening* https://www.mindful.org/how-to-practice-mindful-listening/
- *Listening Builds Trust - Trust Edge* https://trustedge.com/listening-builds-trust/
- *The Barriers to Effective Listening and How to Overcome ...* https://hrdqu.com/communication-skills-training/the-barriers-to-effective-listening-and-how-to-overcome-them/
- *Emotional Regulation for Clearer Communication* https://fierceinc.com/navigate-emotions-wisely-identifying-and-regulating-emotions-for-clearer-communication/
- *Listening: A Key to Cultural Competence* https://mccormickcenter.nl.edu/library/listening-cultural-competence-220823/
- *How to Stay on Topic While Speaking: Tips and Tricks - Yoodli* https://yoodli.ai/blog/how-to-stay-on-topic-while-speaking-tips-and-tricks#:~:text=Active%20listening%20is%20a%20key,prevent%20your%20mind%20from%20wandering.
- *The Role Of Body Language In Communication* https://www.betterhelp.com/advice/body-language/the-role-of-body-language-in-communication/
- *How Body Language Is Informed By Culture* https://www.forbes.com/sites/quora/2023/10/23/how-body-language-is-informed-by-culture/
- *Digital body language: How non-verbal communication ...* https://english.elpais.com/technology/2024-05-02/digital-body-language-how-non-verbal-communication-works-on-social-media.html
- *The influence of emotional intelligence on facial ...* https://www.sciencedirect.com/science/article/pii/S0191886925000029
- *How to Practice Mindful Listening* https://www.mindful.org/how-to-practice-mindful-listening/
- *How Role-Playing Can Enhance Empathy* https://www.psychologytoday.com/us/blog/empathy-emotion-and-experience/202104/how-role-playing-can-enhance-empathy
- *Feedback Loops: The Art of Listening in Effective ...* https://www.linkedin.com/pulse/feedback-loops-art-listening-effective-communication-jay-dhahan-jmake
- *How and Why to Keep a Listening Journal (and a Template to ...* https://flypaper.

soundfly.com/play/how-and-why-to-keep-a-listening-journal-and-a-template-to-get-you-started/

- *How A Two-Minute Communication Rule Can Further* ... https://www.forbes.com/councils/forbescoachescouncil/2018/10/15/how-a-two-minute-communication-rule-can-further-strategic-discussions/
- *The Power of Open-Ended Questions - Minnesota* ... https://mcm.org/open-ended-questions/
- *Reflecting and Paraphrasing* https://counsellingtutor.com/basic-counselling-skills/reflecting-and-paraphrasing/
- *Manage Dominant Voices in Team Discussions* https://www.linkedin.com/advice/0/dealing-team-member-who-dominates-group-discussions-jdlvf
- *How to Develop Empathy: 10 Best Exercises for Adults* https://positivepsychology.com/empathy-worksheets/
- *The Art of Emotional Resonance: A Critical Chapter in the* ... https://simplyvinita.medium.com/the-art-of-emotional-resonance-a-critical-chapter-in-the-manual-of-your-life-57d1d300e4f3
- *Reflective Listening | UNSW Teaching Staff Gateway* https://www.teaching.unsw.edu.au/group-work-reflective-listening
- *Vulnerability in Relationships: Benefits and Tips* https://psychcentral.com/relationships/trust-and-vulnerability-in-relationships
- *Video conferencing etiquette: 10 tips for a successful* ... https://resources.owllabs.com/blog/video-conferencing-etiquette
- *7 tips for effective communication using chat and text* https://livelearn.ca/article/digital-citizenship/7-tips-for-effective-communication-and-etiquette-using-chat-and-text/
- *Media Multitasking and Cognitive, Psychological, Neural* ... https://pmc.ncbi.nlm.nih.gov/articles/PMC5658797/
- *How to Elevate Your Presence in a Virtual Meeting* https://hbr.org/2020/04/how-to-elevate-your-presence-in-a-virtual-meeting
- *How Good Are Your Listening Skills?* https://www.mindtools.com/ai4ff5e/how-good-are-your-listening-skills
- *Master SMART Goals for Personal Development + Examples* https://www.briefblink.com/smart-goals-for-personal-development/
- *Listening strategies | English and Language Arts Education* ... https://library.fiveable.me/english-education/unit-6/listening-strategies/study-guide/tpT6rbaokeqVzm4W
- *Designing Safe and Supportive Physical Classroom* ... https://ca-safe-supportive-schools.wested.org/wp-content/uploads/2023/09/CCSC-Brief_Designing-Safe-and-Supportive-Physical-Classroom-Environments_A-Checklist_FINAL_ADA.pdf
- *Active Listening: Using Listening Skills to Coach Others | CCL* https://www.ccl.org/articles/leading-effectively-articles/coaching-others-use-active-listening-skills/
- *Case Study: Aviation Leaders & Active Listening | CCL* https://www.ccl.org/client-successes/case-studies/helping-leaders-form-deeper-connections-by-building-active-listening-feedback-skills/

- *12 Barriers to Effective Listening & How to Overcome Them* https://hrdqu.com/communication-skills-training/learning-to-overcome-barriers-to-listening-skills-in-the-workplace/
- *Therapeutic Listening | Cleveland Clinic Children's* https://my.clevelandclinic.org/pediatrics/departments/therapeutic-listening
- *Introduction: The Importance of Continuous Learning in ...* https://www.kgcareeracademy.com/post/introduction-the-importance-of-continuous-learning-in-career-development?srsltid=AfmBOorQHqxE2HOgcYZKh7agt DxiyVJqLEl7ionhX-2GLnK02P1nP-Hh
- *The Effects of Your Experiences & Mindset on How You ...* https://www.carolyndickinson.com/blog/the-effects-of-your-experiences-mindset-on-how-you-communicate
- *How to develop a reflective practice* https://thinkingmuseum.com/2021/11/17/how-to-develop-a-reflective-practice/
- *Empathy and Active Listening- Essential Skills for the Future of ...* https://hrs.wsu.edu/empathy-and-active-listening-essential-skills-for-the-future-of-work/